JOHN STEINBECK

ALSO BY KEITH FERRELL

H. G. Wells: First Citizen of the Future
Ernest Hemingway: The Search for Courage
George Orwell: The Political Pen

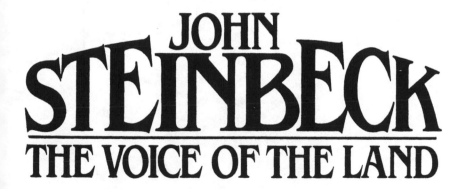

JOHN STEINBECK
THE VOICE OF THE LAND

KEITH FERRELL

M Evans
Lanham • New York • Boulder • Toronto • Plymouth, UK

M. Evans
An imprint of The Rowman & Littlefield Publishing Group, Inc.
4501 Forbes Boulevard, Suite 200, Lanham, Maryland 20706
http://www.rlpgtrade.com

10 Thornbury Road, Plymouth PL6 7PP, United Kingdom

Distributed by National Book Network

British Library Cataloguing in Publication Information Available

Library of Congress Cataloging-in-Publication Data Available

ISBN 13: 978-1-59077-358-1 (pbk: alk. paper)

♾™ The paper used in this publication meets the minimum requirements of American National Standard for Information Sciences—Permanence of Paper for Printed Library Materials, ANSI/NISO Z39.48-1992.

Printed in the United States of America

Designed by Diane Gedymin

FOR JOYCE EARNHARDT

CONTENTS

ONE
SALINAS BOY

THE REGION INTO WHICH John Steinbeck was born in 1902 offered all the diversity of terrain anyone could imagine. California's long Salinas Valley held more than 600,000 of America's most fertile acres. Through the center of the valley, flanked by stands of willow and cottonwood, flowed the Salinas River. Mountains surrounded the valley. To the east stood the gentle Gabilan Range, its Spanish name taken from the hawks that soared in the high sky. To the west climbed the Santa Lucia Mountains, rugged peaks, some of which reached up a mile and more. Beyond the Santa Lucias the land sloped steeply down to meet the Pacific Ocean.

Valley, mountains, shore, sea—Steinbeck could have spent his life within fifty miles of his birthplace and never have exhausted the variety of vistas. In a way he never did exhaust those vistas, for he returned to them both physically and in his writings throughout his life.

Steinbeck's grandparents had come to this peaceful valley across arduous routes. His paternal grandfather, Johannes Adolph Grossteinbeck (sometimes spelled *Grosssteinbeck*) left his home near Dortmund, Germany, in 1856. Grossteinbeck, seventeen at the time, was bound for the Holy Land along with his brother and other members of his family. The pilgrimage began during the Easter season, but by summertime young

9

Grossteinbeck was engaged in more earthly pursuits. He met an American girl, Almira Dickson, whose father was a Massachusetts missionary sent to the Holy Land to persuade Jews to become Christians.

In early June 1856, Johannes Grossteinbeck and Almira Dickson were married. The couple, along with Grossteinbeck's brother, joined Reverend Dickson's farming mission in the desert. The land was harsh, and its harshness had shaped a people who were in some ways violent. Arab nomads raided the mission, killing Grossteinbeck's brother and assaulting Almira's mother. Discouraged, their zeal shattered beyond repair, the surviving missionaries surrendered their dream of converting the Jews. They returned to the United States where Johannes Grossteinbeck became, simply, John Adolph Steinbeck. Trained as a cabinetmaker, Steinbeck felt confident that he could use his skills to support his family and build a quiet, respectable life. After a brief stay in Massachusetts, he and Almira settled in St. Augustine, Florida.

Steinbeck's hopes for a quiet life collapsed with the coming of the Civil War. A son, John Ernst Steinbeck, was born in St. Augustine in 1863. Not long afterward his father was drafted into the Confederate Army. The German-born cabinetmaker accepted his conscription dutifully, however uncertain his allegiance to the Confederacy might have been. Once in gray uniform, however, Steinbeck made up his mind to return with his family to the more hospitable North. When the war ended, he, Almira, and their son settled for a time in Massachusetts. For all his skills as a woodcarver and carpenter, Steinbeck earned only a marginal living in Massachusetts. His thoughts turned once more to moving with his family.

This new pilgrimage, Steinbeck decided, would be practical rather than spiritual. In the spring of 1874, Steinbeck journeyed to Hollister, California. He used money loaned to him by the Dickson family to finance the construction of a mill where grain was ground into flour. The mill proved a success, and within six months Steinbeck had earned enough to send for his family. The Steinbeck mill continued to grow, and the Steinbeck name came to be recognized and respected. The immigrant cabinetmaker continued to add to his holdings, achieving prosperity by investing in land and occasional business ventures.

John Adolph's eldest son inherited a good deal of ambition from his father. In 1890, at the age of twenty-seven, John Ernst Steinbeck set out to seek a fortune of his own. A business-minded young man as skilled at working with numbers as was his father at working with wood, Steinbeck moved to King City, sixty miles south of Hollister, where he found work as a bookkeeper.

Steinbeck's employer was himself an immigrant. Charles Le Roi, a Frenchman who Americanized his name to become Charles King, had less than a decade earlier purchased 13,000 acres of the Salinas Valley's prime grazing land. But Charles King was not interested in raising cattle. His goal was to prove that sugar beets could be grown and refined in the Salinas Valley. Although this plan for producing sugar ultimately failed, King's ranch remained a viable concern, its acres sowed with grain rather than beets. King recognized in John Ernst Steinbeck an exceptional young man and placed Steinbeck in charge of the operation of his mill. Steinbeck threw himself into his work, but not so thoroughly that he failed to notice the attractive young teacher who presided over a one-room school near King City.

She was Olive Hamilton, another child of immigrants. Her father, Samuel Hamilton, was a cheerful and talkative Irishman who had arrived in America in 1851. Whereas John Adolph Steinbeck had acquired his reputation as a sensible businessman, Samuel Hamilton's renown derived in large part from his ability to tell tall tales. People enjoyed talking with him and listening to him talk. Samuel Hamilton was both a farmer and blacksmith, a man accustomed to manual labor who was also the inventor of a variety of labor-saving farm devices. He eventually settled with his family on a ranch near King City.

Born in 1866, Olive Hamilton grew up on the ranch but determined early in her life not to remain there. Ranch life was too isolated, too cut off from society's mainstream. In her mid-teens Olive moved to the small town of Salinas at the northern end of the long valley. There she undertook training to become a teacher. Olive was bright and studious and by the time she was seventeen had passed the examinations necessary for entering the profession. For a time she taught school on the Pacific coast, near Monterey. Olive Hamilton was in her mid-twenties when she transferred back to King City, where she and John Ernst Steinbeck were soon introduced. Their courtship was brief and sensible. They were married in 1891. A year later their first child, a daughter whom they named Esther, was born.

A second daughter, Elizabeth, was born in 1894, the year the family moved to Salinas. John Ernst was once more responsible for managing a grain mill. He was good at his work, finding ways to increase efficiency and boost earnings. Salinas, California, suited John Ernst and Olive Steinbeck. As the nineteenth century approached its close, they realized that they wanted to remain in Salinas for the rest of their lives. Instead of repeated transplantings, their roots were now being put down.

In addition to running their large, turreted Victorian home, Olive Steinbeck stayed busy with community pursuits. Although retired from teaching, Olive remained committed to the arts, to the cultivation of culture. She loved music, painting, and literature, and made certain that her children were exposed to them from an early age. Olive spent a good deal of her time outside the household, serving on community committees and participating in social organizations and women's clubs. Salinas might possess fewer than 3,000 citizens, but there was no reason it could not have a well-organized society. Olive Hamilton Steinbeck devoted much of her energy to the enhancement of that society.

The new century began. With each year the Steinbecks' roots in Salinas grew deeper. In 1901 Olive again became pregnant. Her third child and only son was born at home on February 27, 1902. He was named John Ernst Steinbeck III. Because of his large ears and sharp features, his older sisters nicknamed him "muskrat" or "mouse." His mother, on the other hand, saw the boy as perfect and immediately set about creating for him a childhood aimed at refinement and the appreciation of cultural pursuits. At bedtime she read to him from great books. During the day Olive saw to it that the baby heard fine classical music. She was determined that her son, as well as her daughters, understand and embrace civilization's more noble aspects. She did not waste a moment in establishing a quiet, tasteful, cultured environment for her offspring.

No sooner was John's third birthday party ended than Olive began the boy's education in earnest. Where before she had read aloud stories to him, now she made John point to the words and read them aloud himself. They worked together for long hours on his reading, Olive setting the boy a schedule of daily "classes." John struggled with the work; he would never forget the agony that reading was for him as a small child. He could barely bring the marks on the pages into focus. He could not get them to make sense. Hour after hour his mother insisted that John pore over children's books and fairy stories, over longer stories and novels such as *Treasure Island* and *Ivanhoe*, over the Bible, and even over such advanced volumes as John Bunyan's Christian allegory *Pilgrim's Progress*. John's reading skills improved only slowly, although his imagination was attracted by the fairy stories and tales of chivalry and magic. The classes continued.

John's father saw to it that the boy did not spend all of his time indoors. John Ernst Steinbeck was a quiet and in many ways self-contained man who felt most at peace when outside. He loved to dig in the earth, to prepare beds for flowers, trenches for vegetables. A dedicated gardener who even maintained a vegetable patch outside his office, John Ernst was always planting things. Olive insisted that the children pursue culture;

their father communicated to them the wonders of the natural world. There was great beauty in that world, great power, great danger. Above all, there was variety. During walks along the Salinas River or through the countryside, John Ernst could point out hundreds of different plants, dozens of species of birds. He showed his children the differences and similarities among the plants and animals. He taught the children the proper names of the many types of life that surrounded them.

The Steinbecks retired each summer to the shores of the Pacific, just a few miles away. Despite the coast's closeness, the landscape and life that populated it were wildly different. Trees hung on to precarious perches on the faces of cliffs. Huge waves crashed against the rocky shore. Tidal pools were almost like oceans in miniature. The pools were rich with small, tentacled creatures, with crustaceans and algae. The great diversity of life between the Salinas Valley and the Pacific coast served as another example of the vastness and inexhaustibility of the natural plan. There was, John learned, an order to nature far larger than anything people understood.

Not all of his natural lessons were so grand and philosophical. John Ernst passed on to his children the craft of gardening as well as an appreciation for the larger view of nature. The children were taught how to plant straight rows. John and his sisters learned how to keep weeds and vermin from the garden. In the midst of such pragmatic lessons, though, a sense of wonder could creep in. There were delights to be found in simply working with the soil, feeling its touch upon skin. The children could feel the richness of the earth. They could smell the life within it.

Despite his difficulties with reading, John quickly learned plant and animal names. His father insisted upon precision in the use of those names, as he insisted upon precisely straight vegetable rows and the precise accomplishment of other assigned chores. When John was four, his father gave him a pony, then spent part of each day teaching the boy the proper care of the animal. John Ernst spoke so little that his words carried extra force with his son. John paid attention. Early on, he began acquiring his own skills as a gardener.

Lessons and instruction came close to constituting all of the conversations John had with his father. Even as a child he could sense John Ernst's solitary nature. He would watch as his father silently saddled and mounted a horse, then rode off alone into the hilly countryside. John began wandering off in search of solitude for himself. He enjoyed leaving the house far behind as he searched for secluded spots. From such points he could watch uninterrupted the panorama of the clouds above the Gabilan or Santa Lucia mountains. He might catch a glimpse of a wild rabbit or find the nest of a family of birds. John's powers of observation improved daily.

There was plenty to observe. Salinas's main road was heavily traveled, a dusty thoroughfare that ran the length of the valley. The road led as well to Monterey on the Pacific. Wagons and trucks laden with produce went by continually, bound for the rail lines, reminders of the productivity of the Salinas Valley. As John grew older, he had to go farther and farther to find seclusion. Often those walks took him along the banks of the Salinas River. The river's ever-changing nature was a source of endless fascination. The Salinas flowed in large part underground, fed by reservoirs deep beneath the mountains. In the spring, the reservoirs were filled by rains, the river broad, running full through fields bright with wildflowers.

But when John walked beside the river during early summer he could see its flow beginning to dwindle as the reservoirs were depleted. A good amount of that flow was diverted by farmers to irrigate their crops. The valley's large crop was sugar beets, which were harvested by the ton and processed at Spreckels refinery, the world's largest sugar refinery. The fields and refinery put a great demand upon the Salinas River, and by late summer its flow was diminished to a trickle. In some places the riverbed would go completely dry.

During summer, the nights in the Salinas Valley were often

chilly. The whole valley would fill with a thick fog from the Pacific, drawn over the mountains by the heated air above their peaks. As summer ended, violent thunderstorms would crash over those peaks. The sky grew bright with lightning that illuminated the whole valley. October was often the hottest month of the year and, the river dry, the month when the danger of forest fires was greatest. By November, though, the cooling winds arrived and the first of the winter rains began to refill the subterranean reservoirs.

Sometimes the rains did not come. Drought was one of the great enemies of an agricultural area such as the Salinas Valley. John heard stories of legendary droughts, seasons that had shaped the nature of the valley and its residents. One drought had stretched out over most of the 1870s. Its death toll included more than 65,000 head of cattle. Dozens of farms failed, their owners' hopes and fortunes destroyed by the weather.

Other years, the rains would be too heavy, overfilling the reservoirs beneath the mountains. Floodwaters crashed through the valley. Floods did not last so long as droughts, but they could be equally destructive. During high water, the Salinas River had been known to spread miles beyond its banks, washing away crops, livestock, and homes with its force.

But most years the seasons nurtured the valley. There were always new families to take the places of ranchers or farmers beaten down by nature. The valley attracted people, and its history was one of migrants and wanderers who settled there convinced they had found paradise. The American Indians had been first, followed by the Spanish missionaries, soldiers, and ranchers who'd named many of the region's communities and natural features. The river itself had originally been called the Santa Delfina, then Rio Monterey, before becoming the Salinas.

Blessed by nature, the Salinas Valley was a fine place for an inquisitive boy to grow up. John Steinbeck—watching the fog roll in, seeing the dust in what had been the river's channel, shivering at the might of a fierce thunderstorm—opened himself to all the experiences and lessons nature had to offer.

When he was six, John witnessed natural force at its mightiest. On Wednesday, April 18, 1908, less than two months after John's sixth birthday, Salinas was literally shaken apart. Between 5:00 and 6:00 in the morning an earthquake raced across California. The shock wave traveled at a speed of 7,000 miles per hour. In San Francisco the earth jumped as much as two feet, buildings swayed and danced against the skyline, fires and panic broke out. Closer to Salinas, cliff faces crumbled into the Pacific. In Salinas itself, the telephone exchange broke down even as an operator was in midsentence. The huge Spreckels sugar refinery was destroyed, as were the Masonic temple, the Elk hall, and the Odd Fellows building. A fissure opened in one of the valley's most productive strawberry farms, flooding the land with salt water, ruining the soil. The Steinbeck home survived the earthquake with only minor damage, but John Ernst carried his children through the town to show them the frailty of human constructions against unleashed natural power.

During the days after the earthquake, John saw how people cooperated. The people of Salinas assessed the damage to their town and set to work putting the community back together. It took three days for the rails in the area to be repaired. When the trains were at last able to get through, the citizens of the Salinas Valley put aside their own concerns and sent clothing, produce, beef, and mutton by the carload to devastated San Francisco. Then they returned to their own rebuilding.

That same year, 1908, was also the year John entered school, the lower grades of which were called the Salinas "Baby School." Thanks to Olive's preparation, John entered the Baby School already able to read and write. He had come to enjoy wordplay, and acquitted himself well enough when required to read, but was no bookworm. In his free time John preferred to roam the hills around Salinas rather than rove through the pages of a book. Books had exerted their effect upon him, however. From the fairy stories and romances to which Olive had introduced him, John developed an active, romantic imagination. He claimed that he could see beyond this world, finding in his places of solitude windows into a world of magic and chivalry. His father felt that John's imagination and sensibility were perhaps too delicate and therefore instituted a program of daily talks about "manly" subjects such as courage and pragmatism.

John continued to receive cultural instruction from his mother and, increasingly, from Olive's sister, Molly. Edward and Molly Martin were childless, and they often invited John to spend time with them on their ranch near Monterey. Like her sister, Molly had strong feelings about the preeminence of art and high culture. She lived on a ranch, but instead of cowboy songs its air resounded with recorded operas, which Molly played again and again. John enjoyed his visits with his aunt, accepting her cultural instruction and comment more readily than he did his mother's.

When he was nine, John entered third grade and left the Baby School behind. That year, during a visit to Molly's ranch, John was given a present that changed his life. It was a copy of *Le Morte d'Arthur*, Sir Thomas Malory's fifteenth-century masterpiece, which retold the story of King Arthur, Lancelot, Guenevere, Gawain, the quest for the Holy Grail, and the code of chivalry and honor that guided King Arthur's court. At first the book inspired no more enthusiasm in John than had other volumes pressed upon him by his aunt or his mother. But gradually the pages of *Le Morte d'Arthur* came to captivate the boy. Soon Malory was all he thought about. Never before had he responded to anything—certainly not to a book—with such intensity. The world of *Le Morte d'Arthur* became more real to John than the real world in which he lived. Malory's tales of magic, of holy quests and noble deeds, of valor and romantic love were not simply stories—they were events in which John felt he participated. He could feel the Arthurian age; he could smell and taste it. John even fashioned his play around the Arthurian ideals recounted by Malory: he carried a homemade sword and sallied forth against imaginary villains, fighting always for honor and high purpose. Another magic window had opened for him.

John's commitment to the chivalric code of behavior did not extend to school, however. Early in his education he was something of a disciplinary problem. Easily bored, John grew disruptive when he lost interest in classwork. His caustic comments and outbursts of temper earned him more than one rebuke. His response as he grew older was to draw more completely into himself and the world of his imagination. He had few playmates and, other than his younger sister, Mary, no close friends. That suited John. He liked to be thought of as a loner. He worked at the cultivation of a sullen demeanor. John made it clear that he felt no great love for the people among whom he must live. He was different from other people. Even in grade school he gave the impression that he thought himself better than those around him.

In 1910 the family's fortunes changed. The flour mill in which John Ernst worked closed down. His employers wanted John Ernst to transfer to a mill in another town, but the family's roots ran too deep. The Steinbecks, John Ernst felt, were a Salinas family and would remain one. Rather than seeking a new job elsewhere, John Ernst opened a feed store in Salinas. He adjusted quickly to the responsibilities of owning his own business, putting in long hours and paying close attention to every detail of the store's operation. John Ernst worked hard to build security for his family. He worried about his inability to pass on the virtues of hard work to his son.

By the time he reached adolescence, John had developed as much contempt for the disciplines and responsibilities of employment as he displayed toward schoolwork. Hired to deliver the *Salinas Index* each morning, John more often than not neglected his newspaper route while he sat somewhere, lost in his imagination. He did no better at other jobs, nor could he be counted upon to do his chores around the house. The one thing John was good at was telling stories. At first he told them to his sisters, particularly to Mary, who saw her older brother as something of a hero. Gradually John began telling stories to other children from the neighborhood. His ability to spin a good tale made John something of a leader among the boys his age, although his sullen attitude often worked against his leadership. The stories he told were as richly romantic as anything he'd read. In fact, most of John's tales were based upon his reading. He enjoyed having an audience, yet was at the same time shy about his talent for language and character. Such sensitivity did not fit well in the tough facade he sought to erect around himself.

Seasons passed. There were no natural excitements as great as the earthquake, although the first two months of 1914 saw twenty-five inches of rain fall on the valley. Europe lay on the brink of a major war, but distant political tensions made little impact on the Steinbecks and their neighbors. The Steinbecks received a good many magazines in which the children could read of current events and issues, but it was the books on the shelves of the family library that most closely held John's attention. Nor were contemporary works—or American works—high upon John's list of favorite reading material. The older John grew, the more deeply he was drawn to the past.

His appreciation of the rich language employed by Malory in the Arthurian romances led John to seek the works of other writers who were masters of language and rhetoric. He immersed himself in Shakespeare long before studying Shakespeare in school. John spent hours absorbing the Bible's language—although not its lessons—as well as that of Chaucer and some of the authors to whom Olive had introduced John when he was struggling to learn to read. Those books had bored him when he was younger. Now John could not get enough of them.

John's intelligence and love of literature were not reflected in his grades. His family could not understand how a boy so bright could perform so poorly in school. Not long after receiving a bad report card, for example, John eloquently pointed out flaws in his college-educated sister's understanding of Gustave Flaubert's novel *Madame Bovary*. High school intelligence tests revealed that John possessed a fine IQ, yet it was obvious to his teachers that John was unwilling to discipline that intelligence. He was often late with his schoolwork. He could lose himself for days in long, complex novels such as Dostoyevski's *Crime and Punishment*, but grew bored and distracted after only a few minutes of studying. John Ernst and Olive were at a loss; they wondered what would become of their son.

By the time he entered high school in 1915, John was beginning to consider undertaking a career as a writer. He knew that he could tell stories that held the attention of an audience. He tried to base those stories more and more on his imagination, less upon what he read. The next step was to begin putting stories on paper.

John continued to style himself a tough guy, a loner. While his schoolmates played sports or worked at after-school jobs, John retired to his room where he wrote short stories, poems, and essays. He was, however, reclusive in full view—John carefully positioned his desk before his bedroom window so that his literary labors could be witnessed by anyone passing the house. When he completed a piece he would rush downstairs in search of someone to whom it could be read. His audiences, especially adults, were often unwilling or uninterested, but that did not stop John. He would not accept the fact that people had other things to do than listen to his latest composition. John would corner a neighbor and read aloud until his words drowned out all protests.

He worked hard at his sentences, trying to create rich, poetic images worthy of Malory or Shakespeare. John strung the sentences together into paragraphs that were in turn linked to become stories. He wanted more attention for his work than Salinas could provide and began sending his work to national magazines. For all his projected toughness, though, John was quite shy. He used false names on his manuscripts and put no return address on the envelopes that carried them to editors. It was as though he did not want to know whether his work was accepted or rejected. He never learned what, if anything, editors thought of these early efforts, although he looked for his work in their magazines each month. None of the stories saw print.

Literature was not the only profession that called to him. The Steinbecks' summer home in Pacific Grove near Monterey was close to the Hopkins Marine Station, an oceanographic laboratory operated by Stanford University. The precision with which the scientists at the station went about their work intrigued John. Glass-bottomed observation boats went forth in search of marine specimens that were examined on long tables cluttered with scientific apparatus. Science could be pursued by amateurs as well. The father of John's friend Edward Silliman was a dedicated ornithologist who brought to his hobby of bird watching all the care and diligence of a scholar. John loved to watch Mr. Silliman make methodical records in his notebooks; he watched carefully as Edward's father labeled each bird's egg or feather that he found, preparing them as though for museum display. It was appealing work, and John began to think that he might become a scientist.

Such an ambition, though, required a more resolute approach to academics than did a writing career. A writer needed nothing more than talent, pencil, and paper. Scientists required years of education. John did not completely abandon his hopes of writing for publication, but he did apply himself more thoroughly to his schoolwork. In addition to English and history courses, John signed up for mathematics, science, and Latin instruction. For a while he did better in school and even came a bit out of his solitary shell. During his senior year in high school he served not only as one of the editors of *El Gabilan*, the school yearbook, but also as president of the twenty-four-student senior class. John was no model student, but for a time the dream of becoming a scientist engaged his interest in study.

John's newfound discipline was interrupted by illness. Early in 1917 he caught a bad cold that developed into pleurisy, an infection of the delicate membrane that surrounds the lungs and joins them to the rib cage. John's fever climbed; his breathing grew ragged and painful. He lapsed into and out of consciousness. At last there was no hope for him other than surgery. The operation was performed in John's room. The doctor removed a rib, allowing the pus that had collected in the pleura to drain. For several days after the operation John lay in a coma, but his constitution gradually rallied and he grew stronger. His recuperation lasted for months, with John spending much of that time catching up on schoolwork he'd missed.

He was busy with other things as well. The war in Europe had erupted and deepened. The United States was slowly drawn into the conflict, formally entering World War I in April 1917. After John had recovered from pleurisy, he spent much of his after-school time in uniform, as a cadet. Like his schoolmates—and high school boys across the nation—John practiced military drill and riflery. Cadet training was intended to prepare the boys for the battlefield, but it turned out that the cadets could be made useful closer to home. The military's demand for soldiers left farmers without a ready source of labor. The cadets were pressed into duty. During planting season, John and the other cadets went to the fields at 3:30 in the morning, putting in hours of cultivation before the school bell rang. When harvest season arrived, the school was simply closed and all the students went to work in the fields. The young laborers were paid thirty-five cents for each hour they worked.

The war ended as John's senior year in high school began. In addition to his duties as class president and associate editor of *El Gabilan*, John was preoccupied with thoughts of the future. It was taken for granted in the Steinbeck family that the children would attend college. John was planning to go to Stanford University. But as he approached graduation, John was made aware that the family's financial resources were not large. John Ernst's feed store had not done well, and he finally sold the store as a means of raising tuition money for his children. John Ernst took a job at the Spreckels sugar refinery, rebuilt after the earthquake. Between his salary and the funds from the sale of the store he could meet the cost of sending his children to college. There were limits, though, to how much money he could provide beyond the basic tuition, room, and board. John understood that if he wanted extra money while he was in school, he would have to earn the money himself.

After graduation from high school, John went to work with the laborers building and strengthening transportation and irrigation canals to better exploit the Salinas River. John spent the early weeks of the summer of 1919 feeling his body toughen as he wielded a shovel and swung a heavy pick. His attitudes were toughening, too. The laborers with whom he worked were different from anyone John had ever known. These men, many of them Mexican or Chinese, were not earning money for college. Many of them could not even write their own names. Most of them were immigrants, many of them working illegally in the United States. They were gamblers and hard drinkers, men of violent temperament, whose language and personal habits were foul. It was not uncommon to read newspaper articles decrying the migrant work force as a group of thieves, killers, rapists. Sermons were preached about the dangers of such men.

John had other ideas. At first the canal crews frightened him a bit. But as he grew more accustomed to the hard labor, he also got to know the men he worked with. They talked together during rest breaks. John had been smoking cigarettes secretly for several years; now he brought his tobacco into the open. The laborers shared their cheap wine and liquor with John, and he boasted to his friends in Salinas that he was quite a heavy drinker. Marijuana use among the crews was not uncommon. Most of the crude talk was about sex. Arguments were settled simply, with abusive language and rough fists. There was little status to be had among the workers. None of them owned anything, nor were they overly impressed with anyone who did. This was a world as far removed from the comfortable Steinbeck home as could be imagined.

The summer job kindled John's imagination. Hopes of becoming a scientist began to be replaced by another goal. A stronger-than-ever urge to write came over John. For the first time in his life he possessed a set of powerful experiences on which to base his writing. He could write of real life, as he had seen it, rather than trying to conjure exciting, romantic stories from his imagination. John found the translation of his experiences into stories to be the hardest work he'd ever attempted. He could not stop trying. A day's work exhausted him, yet he would stay up late struggling to find the words that would capture the sights and sounds of life among the laborers. In earlier pieces John had sought to equal Malory's rich imagery and to espouse Arthurian ideals. Now he set himself a harder course. He wanted to make his writing *real*.

John's ambition to be a writer did not impress John Ernst and Olive Steinbeck. It was one thing to want to write, quite another to live the life of a writer. There was no security in that profession, and quite a bit of sacrifice. Why couldn't John pursue his interest in science and continue his writing as a hobby? John would not compromise. He shifted his proposed Stanford curriculum from the sciences to a general liberal arts program. In part to silence his parents' objections, he pointed out that a liberal arts degree offered good preparation for a career as a teacher or an attorney.

John knew that such careers were not for him. He felt like a writer, no matter how poor his early efforts might be. John knew that with time his writing would improve. More important, he had come to a new understanding of the world and the way it worked. For all their roughness, the workers on the canal crews possessed measures of generosity and greed, gentleness and violence, wisdom and stupidity in about the same proportions as the citizens of Salinas. The workers were people, and John wanted to put them on the page.

TWO

STRIKING OUT AT STANFORD

WHATEVER ACADEMIC DISCIPLINE JOHN had acquired during his final years of high school did not accompany him to Stanford in October 1919. The great university was less than four decades old but was often referred to as the Harvard or Yale of the West Coast. Stanford was deliberately created, cultivated, and funded to be a major center of education, but its many opportunities were not for John Steinbeck.

The summer had left him tanned and muscular. At seventeen he stood six feet tall. He smoked cigarettes heavily and spoke of his fondness for liquor and the company of women. John shared a room with George Mors on the first floor of Encina Hall, a five-story dormitory. Mors was also a freshman, planning to become an engineer and carrying a full load of difficult technical courses. John's roommate was well organized and studious, the sort of young man who might be held up as an example of a model student. John was not interested in models of good behavior. Weeks of hard labor with tough crews had made him into his own man. John would make his own rules.

He made certain everyone knew how independent he was. John would not be bound by the expectations or rules the university imposed upon its students. If he did not feel like going to class, he did not go. If he wanted to attend a lecture for which he was not enrolled, he sat in anyway. Class assignments

27

received only the barest attention. While Mors and others studied, John roamed the stacks of the magnificent Stanford library. He read whatever caught his attention. John ignored basic texts upon which an education could be built. He concentrated instead on great and obscure novels, poetry, and works of history. Even that ambition soon faded: by midsemester John was spending most of his time reading pulp fiction. Exciting detective stories printed on cheap paper were more important to him than the university's required reading.

Perhaps aware that their son's attention might wander, John Ernst and Olive insisted that John spend his weekends at home in Salinas. They could keep up with him there and make sure he was properly devoting his energy to his studies. John followed their wishes for the first few weeks of school but soon began fashioning explanations for why he could not come home. His parents thought that he was spending his weekends at the Stanford library. John was actually investigating the delights and temptations of San Francisco, just a few miles from the Palo Alto campus. Sometimes he did stay on campus over a weekend. On such occasions he could always find a card game or a companion to share a bottle of wine. There were far better things to do than study.

John's first quarter results were dreadful. He completed barely half the work required of him, and that with poor grades. Worse, John had become a disciplinary problem in some classes. He acquired among his professors the reputation of being a loudmouth, someone who joked and whispered his way through lectures, disrupting the concentration of those around him. The university made clear that it would not tolerate such behavior for long. John was unrepentant. He was a writer, he proclaimed, although since summer's end he'd done little writing. As far as the professors' complaints, John saw little reason to respond. Everyone should be able to tell that John already knew more than any of his teachers.

His attitude seemed certain to result in early dismissal from

Stanford, but John's college career was rescued by illness. In the middle of his second quarter, John caught the flu. The influenza developed into pneumonia. John's parents, recalling his bout with pleurisy, brought John back to Salinas to recover. John stayed in bed throughout the winter. As had happened during the episode with pleurisy, John's illness seemed to instill in him a new determination to succeed at school. He returned to Stanford in the spring of 1920, filled with resolve. John moved back in with George Mors and set about becoming a model student himself. In May his body betrayed his good intentions. John's appendix had to be removed. He went through the operation and recovery in Salinas, missing the rest of the school year. John had completed—with poor grades—only three courses out of two semesters.

George Mors spent the summer of 1920 with the Steinbecks. John and Mors secured jobs with survey crews mapping the route of what would be the Pacific Coast Highway. They worked in the Santa Lucia Mountains, chopping brush and lugging heavy equipment over rugged terrain. John was too exhausted to appreciate the company of rough men this time. The young men looked to John's father for a way out of the surveying job. John Ernst found them positions in the maintenance department at Spreckels sugar refinery. This work was more to their liking, and they stuck with their jobs through the summer.

John was aware that his parents found more to admire in George Mors than they did in their own son. Mors did little to alter that perception. He spoke frankly with the Steinbecks about John's laziness at Stanford. In a private conversation with Olive Steinbeck, Mors agreed to encourage John to apply himself more fully at Stanford. Mors was equally candid in conversations about John's writing. He pointed out that he never saw John write anything. Where were the stories and poems of which John boasted? All John did was talk about writing. John shrugged off the criticism, but he was a little stung by Mors's accuracy. Back at Stanford in the fall of 1920, John spent more time at his textbooks and also at his own compositions.

His academic discipline gave out first. Mors tried to prod John to greater diligence, but it was no use. They joined the newly set up campus Reserve Officers' Training Corps program together, but John attended only a few drills. Not many weeks of the fall quarter had passed before John began cutting classes again. The university had been built on a ranch owned by Senator Leland Stanford, and there were hundreds of acres of beautiful land in which to escape from classroom drudgery. John was far more interested in wonderful books he could come across on his own than in what he thought were dull volumes assigned by dull teachers.

John stuck to his writing longer than he stuck to his studies. He remained convinced that good writing had to be based upon the writer's own experiences, but his own reservoir of experience was small. John wrote sketches about laborers he'd known. He wrote several pieces about college life, but he could tell before finishing them that such stories were trivial and unconvincing. As the semester proceeded and his grades worsened, John began muttering about leaving school altogether. He would go out into the world in search of experiences from which to create his stories. It was the same approach to writing that Jack London and others among John's heroes had pursued. Experience in the world must precede worthwhile writing.

By November it appeared that John would get to experience the world beyond the university whether he wanted to or not. He could not make his writing do what he wanted it to do. Every sentence seemed worse than the one previous. John withdrew into himself and retreated once more to the comfort of cheap magazines. He had little to say to Mors or anyone else. John stopped making any effort in his classes. Mors was sufficiently concerned to write to Olive, telling her that John was about to be expelled as a result of scholastic failure.

Olive traveled to Palo Alto where she and John had a long meeting with one of the university's deans. The dean did not mince words. He openly stated that John had very few prospects as far as Stanford was concerned. He was willing only to offer John two weeks on academic probation. During that period John could not miss a single class. He was also to be held responsible for all the work he'd missed or failed to complete. After stating the conditions of the probation, the dean ended the meeting. Outside, Olive attempted to lecture John about the embarrassment his laziness could cause the family. She wanted him to understand just how much trouble his irresponsibility had caused. John was not interested in her lecture. He was not interested, he made clear, in Stanford either. He was going to have a career as a writer, and there was nothing at Stanford that could help him realize that goal. He could save the university the trouble of expelling him. He could quit school immediately. Olive wept, and John swallowed as much of his pride as he could. Before his mother departed for Salinas, John promised to obey the rules of academic probation.

He didn't last a week. By December he was fed up with Stanford and its requirements. He made up his mind to leave school. John left George Mors a brief note announcing his intention to ship out of San Francisco. He was bound for exotic China and the world of real experience. He left behind him the stately campus buildings and spent the next few days living in flophouses near the waterfront. John joined the queues of seamen seeking working berths on long voyages. He had no luck. Shipmasters were not interested in hiring a young man who'd never put to sea. Christmas neared and John's financial reserves dwindled. He would not go home. He ate cheap food in dirty restaurants. He did without clean laundry. During the Christmas shopping rush he found temporary jobs in department stores and haberdasheries. When the holidays ended, though, so did the stores' need for extra help. New Year's Day

1921 was particularly grim. Away from family and friends, John felt adrift. His depression deepened. At last he gave up and set out for Salinas.

John Ernst and Olive gave John no lectures about his failure at college. Correspondence from the university made formal John's dismissal. The university would allow John to return to its ranks only if he proved himself more mature. That maturity might come from a season or two of hard, physical labor. John Ernst arranged for John to go to work in the Spreckels sugar beet fields. When he had previously worked for Spreckels, during summer vacations, John had lived at home. Now he would be given a bunk in the fieldhouse where other workers slept. Early in 1921 John left home for the beet fields. He carried with him a new notebook and pencils that he had persuaded Olive to purchase. John was going to show his family that he was really a writer.

He spent most of his time working in the fields. They seemed to go on forever. The sugar refinery started by Claus Spreckels at the turn of the century had become one of the Salinas Valley's largest employers. During peak seasons its labor payroll rose as high as five thousand dollars a day, although the workers were not well paid. The fields were irrigated from the reservoirs beneath the mountains. The farmland was planted with an improved variety of sugar beet, drought resistant and tough enough to withstand the constant winds that blew through the fields. The huge refinery, rebuilt after the earthquake, was a marvel of modern agricultural technology, processing nearly four thousand tons of beets a day, producing as much as sixty thousand tons of sugar per harvest. John found himself rising at first light and joining the Mexican, Japanese, Chinese, and Filipino laborers working with hoes to keep the rows of beets cultivated. It was exhausting labor, work that made a man's back ache. Despite his intentions, John did little writing during his free time. He was too tired.

John got along well in the rough company of the laborers.

He was finding story materials and anecdotes, but he was also displaying a talent for managing laborers. By the summer of 1921, John was made a crew foreman. It was his job to set the pace for the workers stacking heavy sacks of mature beets on railroad cars bound for the refinery. Being a boss was more exhausting than being a crew member. John's initial excitement over the possibility of finding stories in the fields faded quickly as the summer passed. He'd found out all he wanted to find out. It was time for him to do some writing. He quit his job with Spreckels and returned to Salinas.

In town there was some tension between John and his parents. John wrote sketches about the workers, but he could rarely make a piece hold together for more than a few hundred words. All of his stories collapsed long before he finished them. His parents were by now convinced that John truly wanted to be a writer. They were less convinced that he had anything important to say. When they spoke of their concerns, John grew annoyed. Near the end of the summer he left Salinas, and to be by himself he moved into the Steinbeck cottage at Pacific Grove, near Monterey.

John hoped the solitude of the cottage and the splendor of the coast would inspire him to write. Once more, though, he was inspired only to talk about writing. He did much of his talking in Monterey and a good deal of it from bar stools. Writers were supposed to drink, and John did. In San Francisco he'd worn dirty clothes out of necessity. In Pacific Grove and Monterey he wore them because they suited his mood. If he could not write, he could act like a writer, or what he supposed a writer to be—a hard-drinking, unshaven, ragged bohemian, an *artiste* whose difficulties with his work were more important than the work itself.

He carried this defiant posture back to Salinas with him in the fall. At home he simply lounged, unwilling to press on with his work or help with the household chores. Often he left home for days at a time, camping along the Salinas River or carousing with companions of whom John Ernst and Olive would certainly disapprove. Their disapproval voiced itself as concern for John's mental and physical health. By the end of January 1922, John Ernst had had more than enough of his son's bad attitude. John could either seek to cure himself of his problems, or he could get out of the house. A physical examination showed John to be in good health. Whatever was wrong with him was self-imposed. More than than, John Ernst argued, it was self-indulgent. John returned to the cottage in Pacific Grove. As the winter passed, he buried himself in great novels, reading carefully to see how writers achieved the effects that made their works so powerful.

The novels and stories he read seemed more real than any of his own experiences. That was even more true for John at twenty than it had been a decade earlier. Reading a great novel was almost the same as living the novel's story yourself. There were so many elements that had to work together in a novel. In his sketches of workers and college students, John had concentrated on characters alone. Now he was learning not only that the characters must be well developed and believable, but also that they must move through a strong story set in a world that is real for the reader. A great novel, John saw, came as close to duplicating the experiences of life as it was possible for art to come. As spring approached, he began to write again, paying attention now to using physical detail and description as well as to making his characters come alive.

The more he wrote, the more eager he became to have new experiences to write about. John forced himself to stick to subjects he had witnessed himself. He began making long journeys up and down the Pacific coast. He visited small towns such as Carmel. He climbed mountains and hiked far into the wild country at Big Sur. Everything was alive and open to him. All of his senses were alert, all of his energies devoted to observation and to the re-creation of those observations. He kept a journal of his walking trips, recording his feelings as well as describing the sights and sounds he came across along the way. At first most of his effort was focused upon descriptions of the countryside and its features. John hoped to use his writing as a means of coming to terms with his ideas and feelings about the natural world. That world's magic still captivated John.

Walking through the region, John grew angry at the increasing amounts of commercial exploitation that scarred the land. Crews of workers with heavy equipment were carving out areas where developers would erect sanitized quarters for the growing numbers of tourists who wanted to experience the California coast's "natural beauty." Back in Pacific Grove, John struggled for several days to put his feelings into publishable form. He wanted readers to appreciate the natural treasures that were being destroyed. He wanted them to share his anger.

When the long article was completed to John's satisfaction, he attempted to place it with the Monterey newspaper. The piece was rejected, although the editor took the trouble to write John an explanatory note. John's article, the editor observed, was too likely to offend tourists. The irony of the rejection was not lost on John. Newspapers and magazines depended upon advertising for revenue. They were unlikely to publish work that presented unflattering portraits of important advertisers. The rejection was not completely disheartening. John's ambition was to write fiction. He knew from his long hours over novels that writers could cover their truths with a layer of fiction and say things that newspapers lacked the courage to put into type. John took up his pencils again. For a while he wrote brief sketches, but they satisfied him less and less. It was the spring of 1922, and the countryside around Pacific Grove grew gorgeous with wildflowers. John stayed indoors. For the first time he began sustaining his efforts through more than a few descriptive paragraphs.

The nice thing about sketches was their brevity. A quick portrait of a migrant worker or a college professor could be completed in a couple of hours. Short stories, John discovered, took longer. They demanded days or even weeks of labor. That discipline had to be self-imposed, which was hard for John. He did not give up. John carefully created a set of characters, basing them upon families of sardine fishermen he'd observed in Monterey. The community itself he was able to evoke well. He captured the feeling of the night fog upon his characters' skin. He put onto the page the sounds and smells of Monterey's Cannery Row, where the sardine catches were brought for processing. For a plot, though, John had to rely upon his imagination. He structured his story around the effects of adultery, of which he knew little. Still, the harder he worked, the more he liked his story. He forced himself to be ruthless as he approached his words. He taught himself to edit every sentence, seeking to use only the most effective and essential language. When this first story was done, he put it aside and started another. This time he worked closer to his own experience, basing the new story on an incident from his childhood. His pencil bore down on page after page. When one story was finished he started another.

His new abilities at writing fiction gave John courage to try another newspaper article. This time he concentrated on nature, leaving opinion out of the piece. With the article completed, John once more approached the editor in Monterey. His work was again rejected, but this time the editor offered more advice. John was trying too hard to bring the natural world to literary life. John relied too heavily upon effect, too little upon insight and reflection. During the course of the rejection it was suggested that John return to college to study journalism and English. Once he had received a degree he could spend time working on a newspaper to discover whether he was really a writer.

John gave the advice careful consideration. Perhaps he had left Stanford too quickly. He was unaware that the editor had a long acquaintance with John Ernst and was participating in a conspiracy to get John back to school. The editor rejected John's article, but he wrote a letter of recommendation that urged Stanford to reconsider John for admission. John closed the Pacific Grove cottage and returned to Salinas to discuss his prospects. His parents were full of conditional encouragement. They would support a renewed academic effort, but John would have to take a job until he was re-admitted to the university. John Ernst was able this time to find his son an indoors position at Spreckels. In the summer of 1922 John worked as a bench chemist at the sugar refinery, testing samples of beets to see if they were mature enough for harvest. Some of his old fascination with the sciences returned as he worked with laboratory tools and learned lab procedure. As always, John gathered material from experience. Scientists and lab technicians began to appear as characters in his work.

Stanford did not make up its mind about John until summer was nearly over. He would be accepted once more as a freshman, but could not return to classes until January 1923. That would put John behind his younger sister, Mary, who entered Stanford that fall. John did not complain. He arranged to share a room with a friend from his earlier days at the university, Carlton Sheffield. Sheffield, whose nickname was "Dook," was also hopeful of a career as a writer. Unlike John, he found the university to be a wonderful environment in which to learn to write. There were other would-be writers on campus, organized into formal and informal groups. The groups engaged in constant dialogues about literature and writing. Sheffield could put on literary airs as eccentric as John's, but Sheffield's audience was composed of college students rather than citizens of the Monterey wharf. John began to sense how much he had missed, how far behind he was. Dook Sheffield was a senior on the verge of graduation. John, nearly twenty-one, was still a freshman.

John could change that. While he remained high-spirited and defiant—John and Sheffield constructed a mock sacrificial altar in their dormitory room—John brought a new level of concentration to his classes. He did some writing that semester, and quite a bit of drinking, partying, and philosophizing. But he also completed his assignments accurately and on time. By summer he'd dealt with his incompletes and was awarded an A in three of his courses. None of his grades was lower than a C. As summer began John wistfully attended his roommate's graduation exercises. The two had become close friends, and John had opened himself to Sheffield as he had to few others. Suddenly, with Dook leaving, the years of college that lay ahead of John lost their interest.

He did not give up immediately. With the good grades providing some momentum, John decided to take some summer courses. He joined Mary at Pacific Grove where they lived while enrolled in the summer program Stanford offered through Hopkins Marine Station. John took two English courses, continuing to prepare for the journalism degree he'd promised his parents. He was more interested in the marine zoology course he and Mary were taking. During summers as a boy at Pacific Grove, John had been thrilled to ride in the university's glass-bottomed observation boats. As a college student on board those boats, he began to see the unity of all natural life. His instructors showed him how to observe natural life in the wild, far from the controlled conditions of the laboratory. From his study and observation, John began to perceive the interrelationship of living things both plant and animal, whether living in the sea or on land. Everything was intertwined and interdependent. There were ultimately no individual elements of nature—there was only all of *nature*, with humans filling a place in its majestic organization. Zoology and its portrait of the order of life excited John far more than literature during the summer.

He could not sustain the interest nor extend it to other areas of study. Before the summer ended he resolved not to go back to Stanford for the fall semester. He made certain his parents understood that he was making a mature decision this time. John was determined to proceed through college at his own pace, and he insisted on paying the rest of his tuition himself. He was far older than most of the college students he knew. He felt that he was too old to continue depending upon his father and mother for support. John would spend the fall of 1923 working for Spreckels. He knew his way around the intricacies of the lab bench and got along well with the other workers. The chemist's job was far less exhausting than field work, and John had enough energy and time to make a serious push on some writing projects. He lived carefully at home, saving his money and focusing upon his goals. By the time he returned to Stanford in January 1924, he was able to pay nearly all of his own expenses and tuition.

Taking a semester off had not advanced John's position at Stanford, but he had become a better writer during the fall season away from school. Some of the stories he had completed in Salinas caught the eye of the editor of Stanford's campus newspaper, the *Spectator*. John returned to campus in January and the following month saw the *Spectator* provide him with his first publication. The February issue carried a sarcastic short story called "Fingers of Cloud." The story displayed John's fascination with the coarseness of life among immigrants and ranchers. John appreciated the praise the story earned and was already at work on new stories. In fact, he was enrolled in a writing class that concentrated upon the short story. The teacher, Professor Edith Mirrielees, prodded John to greater effort. He needed to give his imagination freer rein, she said. No matter how hard John worked on a story, Professor Mirrielees demanded more. She held up to John and the class examples of great short stories. She spoke of the dedication to craft that guided great writers. John began to see just how large a challenge he had set himself when he decided to write. Throughout the semester he spent hours over his stories. His efforts were rewarded with an A in Professor Mirrielees's course.

John spent the summer of 1924 working once more for Spreckels. He joined the crew of a sugar mill the company operated south of San Francisco. Carlton Sheffield joined John for the summer. They enjoyed each other's company, but the work at the small mill was far harder than at the large, modern

Salinas facility. In the evenings John was too exhausted to work at his writing. With Sheffield present, he at least had someone with whom to talk of literature. One particular story was on John's mind. It was a story about Henry Morgan, an eighteenth-century pirate. John called the story "A Lady in Infra-Red." There were days when he suspected that story might be turned into a novel. The prospect of working for months, perhaps years, on a single piece was forbidding. It was easier to talk literature than to get on with its practice. John decided to skip the coming semester at Stanford, once more under the pretext of earning money for his expenses.

Actually, he and Sheffield had decided to see some of California and Mexico together. They allowed the quality of their work at the refinery to decline. John became surly and argumentative. Finally his behavior grew bad enough to provoke a fight for which he was subsequently fired. Sheffield quit in protest, and the two embarked on their adventure. With the money they'd saved, a long, leisurely trip seemed possible. John and Sheffield launched their trip in high style in San Francisco, both of them celebrating and drinking too much. It did not take two days for San Francisco's bar-and-brothel district to part them from their money. The voyage of discovery to Mexico ended in retreat to Sheffield's family home in Long Beach. Through the rest of the summer and fall John and Sheffield worked at jobs ranging from stuffing envelopes to selling radios door-to-door. There were more lucrative positions available, but those called for greater exertion. The young men were saving their energies for the stories and plays they were writing. By January 1925, when John returned to Stanford, he had accumulated a substantial sheaf of manuscripts.

He knew that although his work was improving almost daily, it was still unpublishable beyond the school newspaper. For now, the school was enough audience for John. He honed his skills in order to hold its attention. Everyone on campus now knew that John Steinbeck was a writer. He even lived the way people supposed dedicated young writers lived. This semester John had abandoned the comfortable dormitory and found a five-dollar-a-month shanty. The place was barely six feet square and had no electricity or heat and no running water or kitchen. John was delighted. He laid in a store of wine-making supplies and christened his shack "The Sphincter." In classes, the English Club, and informal writing groups John read his stories aloud. Unshaven and unbathed, his clothes unkempt, John became a campus celebrity. Students and professors either liked him or loathed him, but no one was indifferent about John Steinbeck. Nor could it be denied that he possessed at least the desire to become a writer. Some of his teachers also thought that John had the talent.

One of them, Elizabeth Smith, herself a published writer of short stories, encouraged John to write a novel. She thought that "A Lady in Infra-Red" showed promise. If John could turn the story of Henry Morgan into a novel, he could probably get it published. By February, John was hard at work. For years he'd seen his father making careful accountant's notes in large, bound ledgers. John worked the same way now. He sharpened his pencils, opened his ledger, and began working on a novel. The effort excited him. His ambition expanded. More than just a novel about a Caribbean pirate, this book would tell the story of a man's life. Henry Morgan slowly took shape as a character. John spent hours doing research for the novel, digging through history texts and biographies in search of the sorts of historical detail that would make the book richer and more believable. As he wrote and revised the novel's opening chapters, John saw that the book would have a great theme as well as a great character. He was writing about ideals and goals, and how life changed and degraded those goals. It was an Arthurian theme, John realized, drawn in part from Malory and other writers he admired. He wrote and revised, filling the ledger's large pages with his small handwriting.

John's grades declined weekly. The novel preoccupied him.

By the end of the semester John was once more in academic trouble. He knew that he was finally finished with Stanford. John dropped all pretense of plans for a career in journalism and informed his parents that he was working on a novel. His semester's production had been transcribed into forty pages of typescript, a good beginning. John intended to give the book his full attention until it was done. This time John Ernst put up no argument. Instead, he offered help. John could stay at the Pacific Grove cottage while he completed his novel. Additionally, John Ernst would send John $20 a month on which to live. The arrangement would last for the rest of the year. Under such circumstances, John should be able to discover, one way or another, if he really had a writing career ahead of him.

The novel was now called "The Pot of Gold." Despite the almost perfect conditions his father had provided, John found himself in difficulty. He knew how to put down the physical details of his story but got lost when trying to give words to his theme. John's manuscript had doubled in size by the end of summer, but his hopes for it had dwindled to nearly nothing. Soon he was writing more letters than fiction. He corresponded with Sheffield and others, telling them of the collapse of his novel. John knew what was wrong with the book. Its author was still too young and inexperienced. He needed to know more of the world. John felt that he had accomplished as much as he could in California. An eagerness came over him to leave the state. His older sister Elizabeth was married and living in New York. John wrote to her stating his intention to come to the city and try to make a name for himself there. He knew that most writers ended up in New York eventually. Now it would be John's turn. The city was filled with magazine and book publishers to whom he could show his work. By submitting his stories in person, John reasoned, he stood a better chance of getting them into print. Exposure to the New York literary community might even give him the confidence he needed to undertake "The Pot of Gold" again.

John spent part of the fall working with his friend Webster Street at a lodge in the High Sierra. The resort belonged to Street's in-laws and was set in majestic scenery. John's mind was on New York. He contacted a Stanford friend whose father had connections with the large Luckenbach shipping line. There was a berth available on the *Katrina*, bound from California to New York by way of the Panama Canal and Havana. The *Katrina* was no cruise ship—John would be expected to work his way through the voyage. That was fine; John accepted the berth and readied himself for a November departure. Before he left, he visited his parents in Salinas. They could not completely mask their disappointment at John's college performance. John Ernst, though, now understood how completely and passionately his son was committed to becoming a writer. He admired the ambition and drive, if not the behavior that accompanied it. John Ernst gave his son a hundred dollars to help support him during his assault on the publishing world. The money lasted only until Havana, where John spent it on whiskey and women. When the *Katrina* docked in New York, John Steinbeck had three dollars left.

THREE

STRIKING OUT

FOR A WHILE THE money did not matter. It was exciting enough just to be in the literary and financial capital of the world. Steinbeck went from the docks to Brooklyn, where he moved in with his sister Elizabeth and her husband. By the end of November he was tired of staying with them and was ready to move out on his own. He borrowed thirty dollars from Elizabeth and found a small room. Steinbeck lived carefully, dividing his time between writing and looking for employment. He was not immediately successful at either pursuit. Onboard the *Katrina* he had resolved to write short stories, but as winter deepened around him, Steinbeck put most of his effort into self-pitying letters. For a while he could not find even a menial job. Only at the end of the year was Steinbeck hired, taking his place among the construction crews building the new Madison Square Garden. Located at Eighth Avenue and Fiftieth Street, this was the third New York arena to bear that name and would be by far the largest. Steinbeck was put to work with the brick masons, starting early each morning and working into the evening. His job was to wrestle wheelbarrows full of mortar or cement to the levels at which the masons worked. The barrows were heavy and had to be rolled along unsteady planks on swaying scaffolding. It was the most wearying, dispiriting work Steinbeck had ever known. When he reached his tenement room at night he was too tired to write anything.

By February 1926, Steinbeck was depressed and considering a return to California. He'd made few friends in New York and met no editors. Even if he could get an editorial appointment, he had little work to show. His one good contact in the city was Ted Miller, a Stanford alumnus who was now practicing law in Manhattan. If Steinbeck could not get his work published, Miller suggested, he might look for a job with one of the city's newspapers, magazines, or publishing houses. That way he could at least earn a living by writing, rather than by manual labor. A similar suggestion came from Steinbeck's uncle, Joseph Hamilton, a Chicago advertising executive in New York on business. Hamilton was a generous man who enjoyed spending his evenings with Steinbeck and with Elizabeth and her husband. They attended plays together and dined in fine restaurants at Hamilton's expense. Hamilton was candid with John. Advertising, he said, offered plenty of well-paying opportunities for a young man who enjoyed working with language. Joseph Hamilton had more than advice for Steinbeck—he offered him a copywriter's job in Chicago. Steinbeck declined that offer but accepted his uncle's help in finding work on a newspaper. Before the month was out, Hamilton had gotten Steinbeck a cub reporter's position on the *American*, a New York newspaper published by William Randolph Hearst. Steinbeck's starting salary was twenty-five dollars per week.

Steinbeck was apprehensive about the job. He made up his mind that the newspaper would not interfere with his more important work. Assigned at first to the *American*'s city desk, Steinbeck displayed no more respect for journalistic conventions and rules than he had for college requirements. Steinbeck flaunted the rules in New York as deliberately as he had in Palo Alto. When the *American*'s copy editors attempted to hold Steinbeck to a simple, journalistic prose style, he grew angry. He had his own way of writing and would stick to it, no matter how wordy and florid his sentences struck the editors at the copy desk. There were other editors in New York in whose approval Steinbeck was more interested.

One of them was named Guy Holt, a fiction editor at the publishing firm of Robert H. McBride. Steinbeck met Holt through contacts made by Ted Miller. Holt looked at some of Steinbeck's short fiction and offered encouragement. With a half dozen more stories, Holt implied, Steinbeck would have enough material to make a book. No contract was offered, but Steinbeck did not need one. He moved to Manhattan in order to spend less time commuting to the *American*'s offices. He did not go to the paper often, spending more time at his own desk. Steinbeck hastily dashed off his newspaper assignments but forced himself to be careful and painstaking with his new fiction. His superiors at the *American* grew dissatisfied with Steinbeck's performance and transferred him to coverage of the federal court, a less important beat. He did no better there and took to calling in sick for days at a time. The newspaper followed Stanford's example and placed John Steinbeck on official probation. He ignored the warning. He was working on a short story collection for an important publisher, and he was involved in a love affair with a Greenwich Village showgirl. The *American* was the least of Steinbeck's concerns.

In May his romance came to an angry end. Not long afterward the *American* fired Steinbeck. For a time Steinbeck considered taking up Joseph Hamilton's offer of a job as an advertising copywriter in Chicago. Steinbeck's uncle responded enthusiastically, forwarding enough money to cover Steinbeck's moving expenses. By the time the money reached Steinbeck, he had changed his mind about an advertising career. The breakup of Steinbeck's romance and his loss of a job were receding into the past. As his bitterness diminished, his hopes for New York success increased. Finally Steinbeck returned his uncle's subsidy. He was meant to be a writer, and the prospects for his career were looking better.

By the end of June 1926, Steinbeck had completed his collection of short stories. He put the manuscripts into readable form and called on Guy Holt at the publishing company. Holt was no longer employed by Robert H. McBride, and none of the firm's other editors were willing to consider Steinbeck's work. Disheartened, he tracked down Holt at the John Day Company, another publisher. Unfortunately, Holt's new employers would not consider a book of short stories by a new writer. Holt commented on the quality of the stories and encouraged Steinbeck to submit them to magazines and to try his hand at a novel. Novels were easier for young writers to sell than were short story collections. Steinbeck accepted the advice wearily. He did not show the collection to other publishers.

Shortly before the beginning of July, Steinbeck found working passage on a freighter bound for the West Coast. He was home before August, but did not linger long in Salinas. He wandered for a time along the coast, visiting Sheffield in Palo Alto, catching up with his friend Webster Street in the Sierra Nevada near Lake Tahoe. Both Sheffield and Street had married. Sheffield had turned to teaching, and his writing was suffering as a result. Street was writing a play, but he had just become a father and his new domestic responsibilities were interfering with his ability to work. Street arranged for John to go to work at the resort owned by his in-laws. As summer ended, Steinbeck and Street decided to stay on in the Sierra Nevada for a while. They would divide their time between preparing the lodge for winter and getting on with their writing projects. Steinbeck was almost ready to try "The Pot of Gold" again. He felt that the time had come to write a novel.

In October, Steinbeck was hired to serve as winter caretaker for another estate in the Sierra Nevada. He would be responsible for sealing the estate's main house against the harsh mountain winter and for repairing any incidental damage that occurred during the season. Steinbeck's job provided a small stone cottage. He would be essentially snowed in by the middle of November. It seemed the perfect situation in which to write a novel with a minimum of interruption. Steinbeck settled into the cottage and set himself a daily pace that allowed for more effort on his manuscript than maintenance of the estate. He felt that he knew Henry Morgan thoroughly. His journeys to and from New York had provided the opportunity to see the Caribbean in which so much of the novel was set. Steinbeck knew that his descriptive powers were up to the task he had set himself. Despite the comfortable cottage and the privacy it offered, Steinbeck could not find the right approach to the novel. The manuscript did not come alive. He was not certain what he wanted the book to say.

As the winter deepened, Steinbeck once more retreated to writing letters and short stories. Every few days he would make the difficult journey, through more than a mile of deep snow, to the nearest community, Camp Richardson. He began mailing out some of the stories he had written. One of those stories, "The Gifts of Iban," was accepted for publication by the *Smoker's Companion*, a newly launched national magazine. The story was a parable in the form of a fantasy. Although Steinbeck accepted the small sum offered by the magazine, he was not pleased with the story. He did not want his own name on the piece. "The Gifts of Iban" by "John Stern" appeared in the March 1927 issue of the *Smoker's Companion*. Its author was by that time twenty-five years old and unwilling to be satisfied with the occasional publication of flawed short stories. As the coming of spring brought his job to an end, Steinbeck realized how much time he had wasted. When his employers offered him the caretaker's job for the following winter, he eagerly accepted the position.

During the summer Steinbeck worked at a trout hatchery operated by the state of Nevada. He spent much of his time clearing streams dammed by fallen trees or rocks. Steinbeck began studying the habits of freshwater fish, drawing contrasts and similarities between them and the saltwater species he'd studied at Hopkins Marine Station. During his free time he buried himself in thick books of biology, absorbing as much information as he could. The orderliness of scientific observation still appealed to Steinbeck, but as the summer passed, his scientific curiosity dwindled. It was replaced by a gathering determination to spend the coming winter's seclusion putting "The Pot of Gold" into finished form. He returned to the resorts at Tahoe but could not stop thinking about his novel. Steinbeck made notes and sketched scenes. His letters to Sheffield, Street, and others were filled with ideas and concerns about his book. He wanted the novel to do so much. If Steinbeck could succeed with his plans, "The Pot of Gold" would tell the whole story of Henry Morgan's life, from callow English youth to disillusioned buccaneer. The pattern of that life would have a point: Steinbeck intended to show how youthful ideals were corrupted and twisted by a life in the world of governments, commerce, religion. The story itself, with great sailing ships, romantic love, piracy on the high seas, was romantic, but its author's outlook was cynical. Steinbeck was still the self-styled tough.

He settled in as caretaker and in September 1927 began his novel once more. This time Steinbeck's discipline held firm. All the years of thinking about the novel, of doing historical research and sounding out themes in letters and exercises, now began to pay off. Steinbeck spent hours at his desk, forcing himself to write three to four thousand words a day. Each work session gave him the strength to approach the next day's stint. He would not allow himself to become discouraged, even when his words rang hollow and tinny. Gradually, with much crossing out and revision, "The Pot of Gold" began to take shape.

The novel began with young Morgan preparing to leave his Welsh home. Steinbeck drew upon his own memories to create Morgan's yearning to see far horizons. At the same time, Steinbeck worked to give "The Pot of Gold" a richness that Malory himself might have appreciated. Leaving home, Morgan must also leave the girl he loves. The Wales that Morgan is so eager to depart is a land of myth, magic, and mysticism. In his opening chapters Steinbeck hints at strange powers of foresight among Morgan's family. On the eve of leaving home, Henry Morgan visits a Welsh wise man named Merlin. Steinbeck drew on one of humankind's oldest such stories, the quest for the Holy Grail. According to medieval legend, the Grail was the cup used by Christ at the Last Supper. In the folktales and stories of bards and mythmakers, of Malory, Tennyson, and now Steinbeck, the Grail became a powerful symbol of the search for life's meaning. "The Pot of Gold" told how Henry Morgan's quest led him only to bitterness and loneliness. Throughout the novel the color of Morgan's life is darkened by his abandonment of the magical world of his youth. Childhood's wonders are replaced by fame, wealth, and power, but all of Morgan's achievements are empty. As he worked, Steinbeck was convinced he was creating a masterpiece.

Steinbeck finished "The Pot of Gold" in January 1928. Upon his completing the book, Steinbeck's confidence failed. He could not bear to reread any of its pages. What in composition had seemed a lush and symbolic language now struck him as overwritten. His symbols seemed grotesque and unconvincing. He closed the ledgers in which "The Pot of Gold" was written and put them away in hopes of forgetting the book. In self-pitying letters he suggested to friends that he might store the manuscript in mothballs as a monument to his lack of talent. For a time he was distracted by work. A heavy snowfall caused a good bit of damage to the roof of the main house on the estate. Steinbeck spent days cleaning up the mess and sealing the roof against further damage. As spring neared, he arranged to work at the trout hatchery again. With part of his caretaker's proceeds he bought a 1915 car that was barely worth the few dollars he paid. Steinbeck began halfhearted effort on another novel but could not make it come alive. Before starting work at the hatchery, he visited Salinas. He returned to Stanford to console Carlton Sheffield, whose wife had recently died. Almost casually, he left Sheffield the manuscript of "The Pot of Gold."

Sheffield was impressed, and his encouragement gave Steinbeck the confidence to show the novel to his former writing instructors. Both Edith Mirrielees and Elizabeth Smith agreed with Sheffield. Steinbeck may not have written a masterpiece, but "The Pot of Gold" was certainly publishable. What suggestions and criticisms the teachers offered were technical and precise. Elizabeth Smith felt that "The Pot of Gold" was too general a title. It lacked drama. She persuaded Steinbeck to call the manuscript "A Cup of Gold." The title change and a few minor corrections were all that the novel needed. Steinbeck's job at the trout hatchery was due to begin during the first week of June. Before returning to Tahoe, Steinbeck mustered his confidence and mailed the ledgers containing his novel to his friend Ted Miller in New York.

Miller responded quickly. He would be happy to submit the novel for Steinbeck and had even mentioned it to several publishers. But first Steinbeck had to put his book into acceptable form. Editors had to look at many manuscripts each day. They could not be expected to squint and strain their way through a long novel written in tiny script on the pages of ledgers. The book had to be typed, and Miller returned the ledgers to Steinbeck. For a while Steinbeck thought that he could accomplish the manuscript preparation himself. The hatchery had a typewriter that Steinbeck was welcome to use. He was no typist, however, and gave up angrily after only a few days' work. Steinbeck's hatchery job paid $115 a month, more than enough to pay a typist to put the novel into presentable shape. A superior at the hatchery introduced Steinbeck to a secretary who was vacationing for a week and a half at a Tahoe resort. Carol Henning was a pretty, dark-haired young woman. Steinbeck and Carol struck a bargain. Carol would type Steinbeck's manuscript at the rate of five cents per finished page, using the hatchery typewriter so that she could be close to Steinbeck should questions arise.

The typing job went quickly. Carol, twenty-two, was terrifically impressed with the novel and its author. She told Steinbeck how much she admired him and his work. Carol was from San Jose, not far from Monterey. She and Steinbeck spoke often of the region where they had grown up. Their relationship deepened quickly. In the evenings they went dancing at Tahoe nightclubs. The typescript was completed shortly before Carol's return to San Francisco where she lived and worked. By the time the job was done, Steinbeck and Carol Henning had fallen in love. When Steinbeck tried to pay her fee for typing the manuscript that was now called *Cup of Gold*, Carol would not accept his money. She was happy to be involved in such a grand project. It was, she let Steinbeck know, her privilege to be associated with so wonderful a book and so dedicated an author. Their parting, early in July, was bittersweet.

Now that *Cup of Gold* was in a form acceptable to editors, Steinbeck returned the book to Ted Miller in New York. Steinbeck worked at the hatchery through the end of summer, completing a few short stories in his spare time. Having finished one novel, though, he was eager to try another. Steinbeck had no novel-sized ideas of his own, but he inherited a likely project from his friend Webster Street. For years Street had worked on a play that had been titled, in various drafts, "Something O' Susie's" or "The Green Lady." None of the drafts satisfied Street, who was preparing to give up writing in exchange for a career as an attorney. Like Steinbeck, Street tried to use symbolism to make large truths come alive. His play was about the conflict between the world of nature and the world of men. Its characters were a California rancher and his family. Since Street was unable to finish his play, Steinbeck suggested that he try to make Street's situations and characters into a novel. If anything came of the effort, it could be published as a collaboration. Steinbeck decided not to seek employment for the coming winter. Instead he would move into the family cottage at Pacific Grove and, with luck, write his second novel there.

As summer ended, Steinbeck visited Carol Henning in San Francisco. Their passion for each other had not diminished by the weeks they'd spent apart. Now they wanted to share every minute; Carol moved with Steinbeck for a few days into a borrowed apartment. She was obviously devoted to Steinbeck and revealed that she wanted to marry him. Carol had no doubts that Steinbeck would become an important writer. She wanted to help him achieve that goal. If they were married, she suggested, they could live on her secretarial salary while Steinbeck wrote new books. Steinbeck's love matched Carol's, but he insisted that he must make a name for himself before he could marry her. He understood the risks that were involved in marriage. Hadn't Webster Street surrendered his literary ambitions in return for the security of a legal career and justified the sacrifice as required by domestic responsibilities? A married writer often spent more time being married—with all of that institution's social and domestic demands—than he did writing. Steinbeck and Carol parted on uncertain terms. She still wanted them to marry in the near future. Steinbeck wanted to forge ahead with his new novel.

Despite his unwillingness to marry, Steinbeck found that he could not work well while away from Carol. Pacific Grove was cold and damp. Fall was turning into winter. Steinbeck accomplished less work each day and finally put the new novel aside completely. Nor did he have any confidence about the prospects for *Cup of Gold.* His depression grew profound. When Carol wrote to tell him that she was devoted to him whether they were married or not, Steinbeck immediately closed the cottage and returned to San Francisco. He arranged to share quarters there with Carl Wilhelmson, a friend from English Club days at Stanford. Wilhelmson was as ambitious for his own writing as was Steinbeck for his. At Stanford, Wilhelmson had beaten Steinbeck in a short story competition. Now he was working on a novel of his own. Steinbeck envied his roommate's wealth of experience. Wilhelmson was a veteran of the war and had traveled extensively. The two got on well, and as winter deepened, they pressed forward with their projects.

During the Christmas season Steinbeck found his funds exhausted and took odd jobs in department stores. He'd gotten quite a bit of his new novel on paper, but he knew that a great deal of work remained. Steinbeck's opposition to marriage and respectability was undiminished, but as his twenty-eighth birthday approached, he decided that he needed more remunerative employment. Carol worked for the *San Francisco Examiner* and was moving up through the ranks of its advertising staff. The though of such a job, with its own routine and responsibilities, did not excite Steinbeck. Regular employment at good wages was necessary for his survival, but he also knew the effect such a situation would have on his writing. He put off the search for a full-time job as long as he could.

The new year began. Steinbeck and Carol had postponed talk of marriage until Steinbeck was self-supporting. Carol continued to believe in *Cup of Gold*, and in January 1929, her faith was vindicated. Ted Miller wrote in excitement from New York that after seven rejections *Cup of Gold* by John Steinbeck had been accepted for publication. Making the moment even more sweet was the fact that the publisher was Robert H. McBride, the same firm that had rejected Steinbeck's short story collection two and a half years earlier. McBride was now sufficiently excited about Steinbeck's work to offer an advance along with the contract. Steinbeck would receive two hundred dollars upon signing the contract and another two hundred dollars on publication day in August. The arrangement implied that McBride was confident of a good sale for *Cup of Gold*. Steinbeck would not receive his royalty percentage of those sales until the four hundred dollars advance was earned back. Everyone was certain that *Cup of Gold* would be a success.

Steinbeck's certainty wore off first. His novel seemed juvenile now, its language and concerns both overblown and pretentious. When friends wished him well with the novel, Steinbeck shrugged their words away. He'd only written the book in the first place to get rid of his adolescent concerns. *Cup of Gold* was not a real novel, he stated. It was the cynical autobiography of an inexperienced young writer. Carol refused to listen to such talk. She saw the publisher's contract as a symbol itself. The contract represented Steinbeck's success. He had arrived as a writer, and now they could resume their plans for marriage. Steinbeck's response was to bury himself in his new novel. He had abandoned "The Green Lady" as a title. Now he thought of the book as "Who Is the God to Whom We Shall Offer Sacrifice?" He wanted to write a mature novel, one that might make readers overlook the flaws in *Cup of Gold*. By the end of summer he and Carol were living together. Once more Carol spent hours at the typewriter transcribing Steinbeck's penciled manuscripts.

In August *Cup of Gold* was published. Steinbeck's contract called for him to receive free copies of the novel, but McBride neglected to send them. Browsing in a San Francisco department store, Steinbeck was shocked to encounter a copy of his first novel. As he examined the book, his surprise turned to annoyance. McBride had commissioned a cover illustration showing a swaggering pirate, the antithesis of Steinbeck's bitter, conscience-ridden Henry Morgan. The publisher had printed 1,500 copies of *Cup of Gold*, but took out no ads. Department stores had the book on display, but bookstore operators told Steinbeck they could not get their orders filled. Steinbeck checked with the reviewers and critics for local newspapers and magazines. He could find no evidence that his publishers had mailed out any review copies. Steinbeck's mood turned gloomy and resentful. He wrote angry letters to the publisher, and to friends. He had maintained for a while that he did not care for *Cup of Gold*, but he felt the novel deserved a better fate than it had received at the hands of McBride.

Cup of Gold received a few indifferent reviews. The copies that finally made their way into bookstores were often shelved with gaudy adventure stories for young readers. No one seemed willing to take the novel seriously, except for Carol whose admiration was now backed with an insistence upon marriage. Steinbeck at last agreed to announce their engagement. His parents came to San Francisco to meet their future daughter-in-law. Steinbeck learned that John Ernst had obtained a copy of *Cup of Gold* and was impressed with his son's abilities as a storyteller. While he would not recant his disappointment in his son's lack of a college degree, John Ernst admitted that Steinbeck's writing abilities might provide the foundation for a career.

Steinbeck had to live while he wrote, however, and soon would have a wife and household to help support. *Cup of Gold*'s poor sales were not helped by the collapse of the stock market in October 1929 or the worsening economic slump that followed the collapse. As the year ended, John Ernst offered to help subsidize Steinbeck's next novel. Once Steinbeck and Carol were married, John Ernst would provide a monthly subsidy of at least twenty-five dollars and more when he could afford it. Steinbeck and Carol had decided to leave San Francisco, but Carol felt sure she could find work wherever they settled. With her salary and the money from Steinbeck's father, they could live carefully until the new novel was finished. By January 1930 Steinbeck's resistance to marriage was worn down. He and Carol were married on January 14 in Glendale, California, with Carlton Sheffield as a witness.

The newlyweds settled in Eagle Rock, California, in the hills east of Los Angeles. Steinbeck wanted to be away from the city and was delighted with the secluded shack he found and rented for fifteen dollars a month. He proudly wrote to friends that the shack was on the verge of tumbling down around him and Carol. They settled into the dubious comforts of their first home, and Steinbeck applied his skills as a carpenter and plumber to making the place more habitable. Marriage interrupted his work far less than he'd feared. He sat at his desk for as much as ten hours a day. Most of his effort was directed at the novel he now called "To the Unknown God," but from time to time he made notes for a series of stories about the Salinas Valley.

By April he had completed "To the Unknown God." He had worked on the novel for more than a year and no longer thought of it as a collaboration with Webster Street. Still, the idea belonged originally to Street, and Steinbeck informed his publishers that he wanted to include a foreword in which he would acknowledge Street's contribution to the book. The terms of the *Cup of Gold* contract gave McBride an option on Steinbeck's next novel, but the publisher rejected "To the Unknown God." Steinbeck instructed Ted Miller to keep the manuscript on the market in New York. He was making good progress on his cycle of stories about Salinas and hoped to have the new manuscript completed by summer. He called the experimental work "Dissonant Symphony" and for a while it occupied his attention completely. Steinbeck was more than one hundred pages into the manuscript when his faith in it faltered. As he wrote to Ted Miller, though, his faith in himself had not slipped. Steinbeck set himself the goal of writing one book a year. He meant to stick to his schedule.

FOUR

DEPRESSION

BY THE SPRING OF 1930, Steinbeck had regained momentum on "Dissonant Symphony." He was, in fact, writing faster and more confidently than ever. Steinbeck finished the long piece in June. "Dissonant Symphony" was more experimental than anything Steinbeck had previously written. In the new work he tried to turn recollection and conversation into a "symphony" of words that would, he hoped, serve to create more compelling characters than was possible in a traditional narrative. "Dissonant Symphony" was not exactly a novel, although its episodes were more closely linked than was common in short story collections. Steinbeck had sought to simplify his prose as well. Rich, textured language was not suited for a story set in California's recent past.

Steinbeck based some of "Dissonant Symphony" on stories he'd heard about his grandfather Steinbeck. He showed the story to John Ernst, who was shocked and angry at its crudeness. Why did John always have to focus upon the base side of life? What had made him so bitter that he could not appreciate life's higher purposes? John Ernst requested that Steinbeck destroy "Dissonant Symphony." Instead, Steinbeck sent Carol's typescript of the story to prestigious *Scribner's Magazine*. *Scribner's* was one of the country's most respected publications, its contents frequently including work by Ernest Hemingway, Thomas

Wolfe, and others among the dynamic new generation of American writers. Perhaps "Dissonant Symphony" would have better luck than Steinbeck's second novel, now called "To an Unknown God." So far that novel had been rejected by Farrar and by Harper & Brothers, as well as by McBride. The economic slump was becoming a worldwide depression, and publishers fell victim to it just as did farmers, bankers, laborers. Steinbeck was aware that McBride was in financial difficulty and did not send them a copy of "Dissonant Symphony."

Steinbeck and Carol planned a pleasant summer at their Eagle Rock home. The place could not be called a "shack" any longer. Steinbeck's ability to work with his hands had contributed scores of improvements in just a few weeks. Carol painted and decorated. By late spring the rented grounds were well kept, the floors refinished, the plumbing in good working order for the first time in years. Steinbeck and Carol spent some of their own money as they fixed the place up. Carol did not immediately seek a job. Both of them were pleased to have accomplished so much so quickly. Their landlord was even more pleased. A dilapidated shack barely worth a few dollars a month had been transformed into an attractive cottage at no cost or labor to him. The spot would be perfect for members of his own family. The landlord asked Steinbeck and Carol to leave. They had only a few weeks in which to vacate the property on which they had worked so hard. The move also meant that they would have to pay a higher rent. At Eagle Rock they had been able to get by on the monthly check from John Ernst and the small sums loaned them by Carol's family. Now Carol seriously began to look for a job. Her carefully cultivated résumé of secretarial, office, and business experience did little good. When Steinbeck and Carol emerged from their romantic isolation at Eagle Rock, they discovered there were no jobs to be had.

Secretaries were not the only ones having trouble finding work. The stock market crash had been merely the first and most dramatic sign of a failing economy. As the months of 1930 passed by, there were other signs of deepening crisis. Farm prices tumbled. Businesses closed. Mortgage payments were missed. Increasing numbers of people found it hard to feed and clothe their families. Wages plummeted to only a few cents an hour, a few dollars a week. Each week saw more and more people living on the streets. There was no place else for them to go. President Herbert Hoover attempted to instill confidence in Americans, telling them that the slump was no real crisis, simply a temporary depression. He was opposed to any legislation aimed at regulating the economy back toward health. Conditions, the president suggested, would soon take care of themselves.

Steinbeck and Carol, at least, could take care of their own needs. They realized that they could not afford to stay in the Los Angeles area. Steinbeck decided that they should return to Salinas. If conditions were no better there, he and Carol could at least move into the cottage at Pacific Grove where they could live rent-free. John Ernst was all in favor of such a move. He was not hopeful about the economy's prospects and did what he was able to make the young couple's way a little easier. In addition to the monthly check, John Ernst began spending a good portion of his free time in Pacific Grove. He and his son worked well together, and they set themselves some ambitious renovations and improvements. They built a fireplace for the cottage, cleared and prepared the ground for a large vegetable garden, and built a small pond that Steinbeck stocked with turtles. Steinbeck added to the Pacific Grove menagerie from time to time. In addition to taking in dogs, he kept for a while a handsome pair of mallards and even an iguana that was trained to walk on a leash.

Employment was still available in the Monterey area. Its sardine canneries and military installation kept the local economy strong even as other parts of California and the country were slowing down. Carol accepted a secretarial position with the Monterey Chamber of Commerce, although she hoped soon to return to the more challenging world of advertising. Her salary was not large, but with help from John Ernst, she and

Steinbeck were able to get by. Steinbeck supplemented their food budget with frequent fishing expeditions. He found and repaired a battered boat, making it sturdy enough to go out after larger fish. Steinbeck and Carol grew adept at catching nets full of crabs, which were delicious when boiled. By the end of summer the garden was yielding fresh vegetables. Steinbeck kept a sense of humor about their tight circumstances. He refurbished a papier-mâché replica of a roast turkey and would bear it to the table with simpler fare hidden in its hollow insides.

As the Pacific Grove cottage took shape, it and its resident author became the focus for local artists, writers, and amateur philosophers. Sometimes dozens of people would show up at the cottage in the evening, after Steinbeck's work was done. Steinbeck and Carol managed to stretch the contents of their pantry far enough to feed everyone. Great amounts of wine were drunk, and by nightfall the cottage would be lively with laughter, discussion, and song. Things were more tranquil on weekends when John Ernst and Olive came to visit. Their visits reminded Steinbeck of how much he owed them. That debt grew with the arrival of John Ernst's check each month. He borrowed from Carol's parents as well. Steinbeck hated the idea of being in debt, but the debt was necessary for him to concentrate upon his writing. A year had passed since the publication of *Cup of Gold*. Although John Ernst was greatly impressed with the novel, no one else seemed to have noticed it. Steinbeck's prospects for additional publication seemed dim. "To an Unknown God" continued to earn rejections. Some of them were complimentary: an editor at Little, Brown wrote to say that when economic conditions improved, the novel might find a place on their list. Such encouragement was small comfort. Steinbeck would be thirty in a couple of years. He was growing frustrated at how little he had accomplished.

His frustration sometimes sent him into bleak depressions. His temper flared at the slightest provocation. He drank more and cursed the dilettante writers and poets who surrounded him at night. Steinbeck and Carol fought occasionally. He did not let his mental depression keep him from his desk, however. Steinbeck allowed nothing to interrupt his work. Whether or not that work was worth doing was the question that weighed most heavily upon him. In the fall of 1930 Steinbeck and Carol visited nearby Carmel, on the coast south of Monterey. Carmel was a community popular with writers and artists. More than a few of its writers earned good livings turning out detective, western, and romance stories for pulp magazines. They boasted of their incomes, of the number of pages they could produce in a day. Pulp writing demanded no talent, no insight, no reflection. A good pulp story was all action and lurid description. For a career in the pulps, Steinbeck realized, it was more important to be able to type than to be able to write.

The pulp writers' cynicism made Steinbeck's gorge rise. Their attitudes, work, and success mocked all of the dedication and craft that Steinbeck struggled to maintain. He reserved his anger and decided to convert it into work. Steinbeck would beat the pulp writers at their own game. Back in Pacific Grove he threw aside the pages of a new novel, cleared his desk, and in nine days wrote a sixty-thousand-word detective novel. He called the story "Murder at Full Moon" and packed its pages with every plot device he could think of. When he finished the story, he immediately began typing it himself. The job took two weeks. When he was done, Steinbeck was convinced he had a sure sale. He could not bear to think of the novel and kept its composition a secret. He signed the title page with a new pseudonym, "Peter Pym," and mailed the typescript to Ted Miller. Steinbeck hated "Murder at Full Moon" and what it represented, but he hoped for a quick sale. He and Carol needed the money.

In addition to debts owed his and Carol's parents, Steinbeck had dental bills to pay. For years he had neglected to take care of his teeth, and as a result they were in terrible shape. Steinbeck's mouth hurt constantly, but he could not afford to have all of the necessary work done at once. When he had money, or could borrow, he paid a portion of his dental bills and had a bit more work done on his teeth. He was in the dentist's waiting room that fall when he met Edward F. Ricketts, a marine biologist who lived in Monterey. Even in their first brief conversation, Steinbeck and Ricketts realized they had a great deal in common.

Ricketts was five years older than Steinbeck. Like Steinbeck, Ricketts had left college without benefit of a degree. Ricketts considered himself a student of *all* knowledge and delighted in drawing on his wide range of reading. At the University of Chicago in the early 1920s, Ricketts was a student of W. C. Allee. Allee lectured on ecology—a daring new vision of the universe that had at its center the idea that all of life was interrelated. Allee's theories became Ricketts's own, and after leaving the university, he applied himself to private study of biology, zoology, and natural philosophy. Marine biology particularly fascinated him. Ricketts could extend his studies of marine animals, and specifically those living in the tidal pools along the Pacific coast, to embrace all of life, including human life. In 1923 Ricketts came to Monterey and founded Pacific Biological Laboratories.

The company collected, identified, and distributed marine specimens to other labs and to schools and universities. Ed Ricketts could not have found a better way to support himself. The collecting itself was pleasant. During his expeditions after baby octopus or mollusks or any of the other species with which the coast bristled, Ricketts made careful scientific observations and records. He kept detailed notebooks and worked at converting his findings into scientific treatises. Pacific Biological Laboratories did not generate a large income, but Ricketts made enough to cover living expenses and support his research. Ricketts spent what extra money he had on books. He was justifiably proud of the large, specialized, and comprehensive library of marine references and journals that he assembled in his lab.

For all of his devotion to science, Ricketts was no se-
questered scholar. He was well known on the Monterey waterfront, a sort of celebrity among those who lived on Cannery Row.
His lab was the site of frequent parties at which Ricketts drank
more than anybody else. He was a handsome, bearded man
whom women found attractive. Ricketts enjoyed the company of
women and got along well with them. He could be equally
comfortable in the company of a college-educated woman or a
prostitute from Cannery Row. He was his own man, in his
approach to love as well as to science. Ed Ricketts became the
best friend John Steinbeck ever had.

By January 1931, Steinbeck was a daily visitor to Pacific
Biological Laboratories. He and Ricketts were good talkers, and
their discussions went on for hours. Ricketts was impressed with
Steinbeck's artistic commitment and discipline. The marine biologist argued, though, that Steinbeck should be writing about the
people of Monterey whom he knew so well. If Steinbeck wanted
to write about middle-class citizens, Ricketts suggested, Monterey had them. But Steinbeck would also be doing well to write
about the colorful citizens of Cannery Row. The waterfront was
populated by Portuguese-descended fishermen, by the cannery
workers, and by the prostitutes and barkeeps who made their
living from the simple but not necessarily simple-minded fishermen. The hills around Monterey were also filled with likely
subjects for stories. From Ricketts, and from a schoolteacher
named Susan Gregory, Steinbeck heard of the community of
paisanos, as they called themselves, outside Monterey. *Paisanos*
spoke Spanish, although their ancestry included American Indians, Portuguese, and Italians. Their approach to life was gentle, and there were many good stories to be told about them.

Steinbeck listened to the advice but did not act upon it. He
was trying to find a way to write about the people he was most
interested in. He had tried once to write as others recommended. The result had been "Murder at Full Moon," which
had been rejected by the pulps. In the spring he got word, after

nearly a year of waiting, that *Scribner's Magazine* was rejecting "Dissonant Symphony." Nobody wanted "To an Unknown God." The rejections could not have come at a more difficult time. Early in the year Carol had finally grown tired of working at clerical jobs to support Steinbeck's writing. She wanted a career of her own and had gone into partnership with another woman, opening an advertising agency. One of their first clients was a would-be poet who paid $10 a month for the agency to create publicity aimed at increasing the sales of her poems. Steinbeck appreciated the irony, but he was also aware that Carol's business put a strain on their tight budget. He needed to make a sale.

Ted Miller wrote from New York. For years he had enthusiastically shown Steinbeck's manuscripts to publishers. Miller was convinced that Steinbeck had a strong career ahead. He had seen firsthand the improvement in the works since *Cup of Gold.* Miller was now concerned that Steinbeck might be missing sales because he was not well represented in New York. It was time, he wrote, for Steinbeck to acquire the services of a reputable literary agency. An agent could make submissions more professionally than could Miller. For one thing, editors knew the names of the leading literary agents: They were accustomed to dealing with agents and might take Steinbeck's manuscripts more seriously if they bore an agency's endorsement. Carl Wilhelmson, Steinbeck's Stanford friend, seconded Miller's opinion. Wilhelmson recommended that Steinbeck send his work to McIntosh & Otis, one of New York's most respected literary agencies.

For a while Steinbeck hesitated. He was filled with doubt. An agent would provide, at the least, a professional reading of his work. But there was the chance that an agent would respond as negatively as had editors. Steinbeck was not certain he could survive such a response. He'd made less than five hundred dollars from a decade of hard writing that included publishing a novel. He was twenty-nine years old and still dependent upon his parents for financial support as well as for a roof over his head. He had only vague ideas about future projects and had worked only fitfully since completing "Murder at Full Moon." Steinbeck and Carol were not getting along well, and he feared that a rejection by an agent might be a death blow to what hopes they had remaining. Steinbeck's hesitation proved more nerve-wracking than his fears. He told Ted Miller to send his man-uscripts—including "Murder at Full Moon" to Mavis McIntosh at McIntosh & Otis.

McIntosh was in partnership with Elizabeth Otis. They had founded their agency in 1928 and in two years had established a good reputation. Mavis McIntosh and Elizabeth Otis were re-spected for the quality of their clients and for hard work on their authors' behalf. McIntosh focused her attention on marketing novels written by agency clients. Elizabeth Otis specialized in placing short stories with magazines. Both were alert for new talent, and Mavis McIntosh responded quickly to Steinbeck's submissions. She felt that Steinbeck showed a great deal of promise. While she could not guarantee to sell his current work, she encouraged him to increase his production of new stories. She felt that Steinbeck would be most successful if he concen-trated on realistic stories about contemporary California. He might also give some thought to writing new murder mysteries.

Steinbeck was not interested in writing new mysteries. He was intrigued by McIntosh's suggestion that he write about the contemporary scene. McIntosh's advice in some ways echoed that of Ed Ricketts, Sue Gregory, and Carol. Except for a few forgettable short stories, Steinbeck had avoided writing about the present. *Cup of Gold* was deliberately historical. "Murder at Full Moon" was set in the present, but it was no good. "To an Unknown God" could have been set in any period. That novel's story of a farmer's love of land was timeless, as were its themes—the richness of natural life, the impermanence of human con-structions. Those were themes that Steinbeck wanted to explore again in his work, but he was not certain how to adapt them to contemporary settings. His interest, as he pointed out to Ed

Ricketts, was still directed toward writing about gods, heroes, and kings who obeyed systems of ideals. Malory remained central to Steinbeck's thoughts. He wanted to write works like *Morte d'Arthur*. He wanted to use his writing to illuminate his philosophy.

In conversation with Ed Ricketts, Steinbeck's philosophical horizons broadened almost daily. Steinbeck absorbed Ricketts's ecological approach to nature and the place of humans in nature. The concept that there was only one organism and that that organism was all of the universe excited Steinbeck greatly. When he was not writing he could often be found immersed in a book of biology or accompanying Ricketts on an expedition to a tidal pool. In the self-contained universe of the pool was reflected all of the struggle for life on earth. Steinbeck had understood that since childhood. Now, with Ricketts as teacher, he began his own systematic study of the natural world. As he saw more clearly the patterns by which individual organisms fit together to form large aggregations of life, Steinbeck began to conceive an idea for a new book.

Like the unpublished "Dissonant Symphony," Steinbeck's new effort was going to fall somewhere between being a novel and being a short story collection. He wanted to tell the story of an agricultural valley through loosely linked portraits of the people who lived in the valley. It would be an *ecological* approach to fiction. Each of the stories would be linked to the others, but each would also be an individual entity. Steinbeck took as his literary model the Italian Giovanni Boccaccio, whose fourteenth-century masterpiece, *Il Decamerone*, consists of a hundred separate short stories. *The Decameron's* loose structure allowed Boccaccio to tell both humorous and tragic stories, linking them into an epic. If Steinbeck could accomplish half as much as Boccaccio, he would have a book whose whole was far greater than its parts.

By the end of the summer of 1931, Steinbeck was deep into the series of stories. He called his book *The Pastures of Heaven*.

Mavis McIntosh was not excited about the commercial prospects for the project, but Steinbeck refused to be discouraged. He accepted the fact that he might never enjoy large literary success. He was no longer willing even to consider writing projects undertaken solely for money. Steinbeck was after something new. He boldly told friends that he was developing a new way of writing books. Steinbeck considered each of the stories in *The Pastures of Heaven* to be a novel in itself. All the stories together made something larger than just a novel. No straightforward narrative, Steinbeck argued, could create a world so completely. Steinbeck shuffled and rearranged the order of the stories, placing them in counterpoint to each other as a means of further increasing their effectiveness. The work was as satisfying as any writing he had done. Steinbeck was able to lose himself in the creation of *The Pastures of Heaven* and forget that his marriage was going sour.

Carol's advertising firm was not faring well. The Steinbecks went deeper into debt every month, yet Steinbeck still would not take a job. Often after work Carol joined her husband at Ricketts's laboratory, but just as often she found herself having to cook for a cottage full of Steinbeck's literary and drinking companions. When his parents came for their weekend visits, Steinbeck and Carol had to sleep on the porch. After a few glasses of wine Steinbeck might declaim loudly that he was in the process of creating a literary movement that was centuries ahead of its time, but that claim did not help pay the couple's bills. When Steinbeck finished *The Pastures of Heaven* late in 1931, he was exuberant, even though Mavis McIntosh was reserved about the manuscript. The Great Depression was deepening, and publishers were more leery than ever of short story collections, no matter how innovative they might be.

In January *Pastures* received its first rejection. It had been read by editors at Morrow, but they failed to see the philosophy that underlay the book's unusual construction. Carol's business was on its last legs. Neither rejection nor marital tension interrupted Steinbeck's production. The composition of *The Pastures of Heaven* had taught him more about the craft of writing than had all of his other efforts combined. He felt for the first time that he knew what he wanted to see and possessed the skills to say it clearly. Filled with creative energy, Steinbeck returned to his second novel, "To an Unknown God." It read as though it had been written by an untalented stranger. The prose was awful, the philosophy sophomoric. As he completed *The Pastures of Heaven*, Steinbeck began a complete revision of "To an Unknown God."

Steinbeck had grown a great deal since the previous draft of the novel. The story still excited him. Steinbeck's central character was Joseph Wayne, a Vermont farmer who joins the westward movement and settles in central California. Drawing in part on family history, but more deeply on his developing philosophy, Steinbeck brought both Joseph Wayne and his California homestead to life. The land was as central a character to the novel as was Joseph Wayne. Arriving at his property early in the novel, Joseph Wayne is almost overwhelmed:

"As he looked into the valley, Joseph felt his body flushing with a hot fluid of love. 'This is mine,' he said simply, and his eyes sparkled with tears and his brain was filled with wonder that this should be his. There was pity in him for the grass and the flowers; he felt that the trees were his children and the land his child. For a moment he seemed to float high in the air and to look down upon it. 'It's mine,' he said again, 'and I must take care of it.'"

Joseph Wayne's love of his land is at once practical, religious, and sexual. Steinbeck kept his discussions with Ed Ricketts in mind as he worked in his ledgers. For all of his new ideas about fiction and philosophy, Steinbeck could not forget his oldest goals. He wanted to make his story magical, a romance in its own way. When Joseph receives a letter from his brother Burton, telling of their father's death in Vermont, Joseph does not mourn.

"His mind was inert and numb, but there was no sadness in him. He wondered why he was not sad. Burton would reproach him if he knew that a feeling of joy and welcome was growing up in him. He heard the sounds come back to the land. The meadowlarks built little crystal towers of melody, a ground squirrel chattered shrilly, sitting upright in the doorway of his hole, the wind whispered a moment in the grass and then grew strong and steady, bringing the sharp odors of the grass and of the damp earth, and the great tree stirred to life under the wind. Joseph raised his head and looked at its old, wrinkled limbs. His eyes lighted with recognition and welcome, for his father's strong and simple being, which had dwelt in his youth like a cloud of peace, had entered the tree.

"Joseph raised his hand in greeting. He said very softly, 'I'm glad you've come, sir. I didn't know until now how lonely I've been for you.' The tree stirred slightly. 'It *is* good land, you see,' Joseph went on softly. 'You'll like to be staying, sir.' He shook his head to clear out the last of the numbness, and he laughed at himself, partly in shame for the good thoughts, and partly in wonder at his sudden feeling of kinship with the tree. 'I suppose being alone is doing it . . . I'll have the boys come out to live. I am talking to myself already.' Suddenly he felt guilty of treason. He stood up, walked to the old tree and kissed its bark."

The split between Joseph Wayne's profound worship of the natural world and the difficulty of keeping that worship alive in the midst of destructive civilization gave Steinbeck a strong story. Joseph invites his brothers to live in California with him, setting the stage for conflicts and tension. Steinbeck called the new version *To a God Unknown*. As he got deeper into the book, he incorporated a great drought into the story. Each page carried Steinbeck further from the previous drafts, closer to the creation of a novel he could be proud of. He joked that the manuscript sometimes reminded him of a fine automobile whose frame was in good shape, but whose engine needed major repairs. Steinbeck surrounded himself with his book's parts and set to work.

The drought that was central to his novel was based upon a real one that California suffered in 1931. By January 1932, that drought was ended. In February, Steinbeck's professional drought came to a close when Mavis McIntosh wired to tell him that *The Pastures of Heaven* was going to be published. In fact, the novel had been bought after only three days' consideration by Robert Ballou, an editor for Jonathan Cape & Harrison Smith. Cape & Smith was the American subsidiary of Jonathan Cape, Ltd., a respected English publishing house. Ballou was excited enough about Steinbeck's talent to offer a contract not only for *The Pastures of Heaven*, but also for Steinbeck's next two books. McIntosh's telegram arrived on Steinbeck's thirtieth birthday and was the best present he'd ever received. Carol's advertising agency had finally succumbed to the worsening economy. She was earning fifty dollars a month working part-time for Ed Ricketts at Pacific Biological Laboratories, but she and Steinbeck still could not catch up with their debts. It had seemed ridiculous even to dream of getting financially ahead. The money from *The Pastures of Heaven* would be most welcome.

Steinbeck had barely returned the contracts to Cape & Smith when he learned that the publisher had gone bankrupt. It was customary in the publishing industry for editors to carry ongoing projects with them when they changed publishers. Robert Ballou took the contracts for *Pastures* and for Steinbeck's future work with him when he joined the Brewer, Warren, and Putnam publishing firm. *The Pastures of Heaven* by John Steinbeck was set to appear in the fall. Steinbeck did not allow himself to grow too excited. He refused to count on his new publisher's surviving the Great Depression long enough to get *Pastures* on the market. It would be enough if they lasted long enough to pay the book's advance. Using his contract as collateral, Steinbeck borrowed money from friends. Indebtedness pleased him no more than ever, but he could not interrupt his progress on *To a God Unknown*. Steinbeck remained proud of *The Pastures of*

Heaven, but he was coming to see it as a transitional book. Now he was working on the real thing. Steinbeck had broken through to one of his long-standing goals. Joseph Wayne lived on the pages of *To a God Unknown*, a godlike character, a hero.

For all his concentration, Steinbeck was not completely cut off from the external world. He and Carol were making an effort to restore some tranquillity to their marriage. Steinbeck took occasional breaks from his ledger to accompany Ed Ricketts and Carol on specimen-gathering trips. He learned the lore of the littoral, that region of the shore between high tide and the continental shelf. Buffeted by wave and tide, the littoral teemed with life that had adapted to its environment. An increasingly serious amateur naturalist, Steinbeck paid close attention to the collection and examination of specimens. In Monterey the discussion sessions at Ricketts's lab were frequently joined by Joseph Campbell, a scholar at work on *The Masks of God*, an enormously ambitious study of mythology throughout human history. Ricketts and Campbell guided Steinbeck through scientific and philosophical literature. Steinbeck's reading grew systematic. He took notes, played with ideas, looked for ways to incorporate his reading and reflection in his work.

The larger world pressed in as well. By late spring, Carol's job at Pacific Biological Laboratories came to an end when Ricketts ran short of funds. She was ready to leave Pacific Grove, despite their poverty. In July they scraped together enough money for a move. Steinbeck and Carol traveled south again, returning to the Los Angeles area. As they drove, they saw how much more serious the problem of the homeless had become. Now there were whole communities of the dispossessed. People were living in ragged shanties improvised out of cardboard, twigs, papers, and tin cans. Conditions in such places were desperate at best. The communities came to be known as "Hoovervilles" after the president. Hoover continued to insist that it was not the government's role to regulate the economy. There was talk, though, of a final breakdown in American currency. Some states were already issuing their own money.

Steinbeck and Carol settled in Montrose. *To a God Unknown* remained the object of Steinbeck's greatest efforts, but he was also eager to do some work that might sell more quickly. He wrote a few short stories and even gave fleeting thought to trying pulp fiction again. For a while during the summer Steinbeck worked on a play but broke off to return to the story of Joseph Wayne. He checked the galleys for *The Pastures of Heaven*, but let the publishers know how reticent he was to become involved in publicizing the book. For all of his bold posturing as a writer in his youth, Steinbeck now dreaded the thought of giving interviews. He disliked the idea that biographical information about an author might help the sales of his book. Books, he felt, should succeed on their own merits, not on publicity. He was pleased finally to receive part of the advance due him for *Pastures*; yet he was not hopeful of the book's earning much money.

The Pastures of Heaven appeared in the fall. The book was not widely reviewed, nor were the reviews exciting. Some critics implied that Steinbeck showed promise, but they also stated that *The Pastures of Heaven* was a minor work. Brewer, Warren, and Putnam went bankrupt not long after publication day. Steinbeck and Carol were living in a place not much better than a Hooverville, stretching John Ernst's monthly assistance as far as they could. The marriage again grew tense. Steinbeck applied himself fully to his novel, ignoring his personal circumstances as much as he could. He built the end of the book to a dramatic peak, as Joseph Wayne's land lies dying in a drought. Joseph's communion with his land becomes complete. He offers a sacrifice—a calf—to the land, but knows that he must do more. Steinbeck constructed a symbolic ending that was powerful and moving.

Steinbeck completed his novel early in 1933. By February the manuscript was typed, but Steinbeck had to borrow money to pay the book's postage to New York. Robert Ballou was in the process of launching his own publishing house, and McIntosh & Otis forwarded *To a God Unknown* to him. Steinbeck had spent nearly five years on the book since its beginnings as a collaboration with Webster Street. Now the book was wholly his own and would bear only Steinbeck's name. He felt that he had accomplished a great deal with the book, both as fiction and as philosophy. He also knew, though, that such an unusual novel stood little chance of large sales. Ballou agreed with Steinbeck's glum assessment, but planned to publish anyway. Publication would not take place until Ballou's financing was more secure. There was no way to tell when that would be. As if to remind Steinbeck of his insignificance, Los Angeles was shaken by an earthquake not long after the manuscript was mailed.

In March, Steinbeck and Carol were called back to Salinas. Olive's health was failing and she was hospitalized. For weeks Steinbeck sat at her bedside in the hospital. He tried to do some work, but his mother was disturbed by the sound of Steinbeck's pencil on paper. Steinbeck put aside his work and simply sat, thinking. Late in the spring a stroke left Olive paralyzed. Steinbeck's thinking grew more focused. His mother's cells were in rebellion, with the result that she had ceased to function as an individual. He began to think of individuals as cells. No individual could exist separate from the group that was composed of all individuals, yet the group continued to exist despite the death or incapacity of any individual. As Steinbeck sat at his mother's bedside, he thought of the logic of the group. It seemed as though groups had minds of their own, over and above such aspects of society as laws or morality. Groups possessed an unspoken consciousness. Along the coast such a consciousness could be perceived in the structures of coral, built by billions of tiny creatures acting together. In animals the group mind could result in suicidal behavior such as the lemmings' mad, mass migration to hurl themselves to death in the sea. In humans the group mind could produce a lynch mob capable of actions no individual would pursue. The group had not only its own mind, but also its own virtually unstoppable will.

The ideas seized and shook Steinbeck. Here was a concept that could serve as the basis for any number of serious works of fiction and nonfiction. Steinbeck knew that he was onto something that would give his work a scope and purpose that few contemporary writers had the courage to attempt. He drew upon his knowledge of history to give his theory a name. Roman legions, on going into battle, formed a unit called a *phalanx*. In a phalanx all of the legionnaires were drawn closely together, their shields touching until the body of soldiers was communally armored. A phalanx moved and fought as one entity, capable of far greater destruction than its individual soldiers could wreak. Like the human body, a phalanx was composed of individual cells, but all of the cells together made more than a simple aggregation or collection. Steinbeck wrote a short essay on the subject, "Argument of Phalanx," in which he outlined his new view of the universe. When the galleys of *To a God Unknown* arrived, he saw in his second novel the seeds of the ideas that were now furiously germinating. The book was a breakthrough in Steinbeck's writing style as well. Its lushness and poetry did not seem overdone as in *Cup of Gold*. Steinbeck could read his sentences, descriptions, and dialogue without embarrassment.

By June it was clear that Olive would not recover from the paralysis. She was moved back to the Salinas house. John Ernst was frail himself, in no condition to undertake the demanding care that Olive required. Steinbeck's sisters now had families of their own and could not abandon their domestic responsibilities. Steinbeck and Carol, childless, were elected to stay in Salinas to nurse Olive through what everyone knew would be her final illness. Steinbeck was thirty-one years old. After years of being at least partially supported by his parents, he now found himself back in his childhood home. He had published two books, with a third on its way, yet had earned less than a thousand dollars from all of his sales combined. The move to Salinas put pressure on Carol and on their marriage. Steinbeck struggled to keep his writing at the center of his attention. He sought to establish a rhythm by which he could get some real work done.

At first there was no time to do anything but care for his mother. Olive could barely speak, and what words she managed were further garbled by advancing senility. The stroke had left her with little control over her functions. She soiled as many as a dozen sheets a day, which Steinbeck washed and Carol ironed. Carol worked at office jobs and returned home to attend to the kitchen and most of the housekeeping. When the cleaning was done, she typed up her husband's manuscripts. Steinbeck helped, too, dealing with the upkeep and maintenance of the house. When he found time, he prowled through old Bibles and family records, absorbing as much as he could of the history of the Steinbeck and Hamilton families, learning about the part his ancestors had played in settling and developing the Salinas Valley. He pored over family medical books, the heavily thumbed sections of which told him which illnesses and maladies had been most common. Steinbeck listened to his father's reminiscences, getting a feel for the valley as it had been. Steinbeck meant to know everything about the area. Someday he would write about it.

The household gradually settled down, and Steinbeck once more began keeping regular hours at his ledger. He started a story about a Salinas Valley ranch near the turn of the century. His characters were a farm couple named Tiflin, their son Jody, and their ranch hand Billy Buck. The story gathered momentum more quickly than anything Steinbeck had written in years. He held back his urge to philosophize. The events and characters in the story must speak for themselves, in sentences as free of pretension as was life on a ranch. Steinbeck's story dealt with Jody's colt, which was named Gabilan after the mountains on the edge of the valley. He called the story "The Red Pony."

┌─ FIVE ─┐
SUCCESS AND CONTROVERSY

WHEN THE STORY WAS finished, it was ten thousand words long. After the excitement of writing had worn off, Steinbeck thought "The Red Pony" was sentimental, even foolish. He mailed the typescript to McIntosh & Otis anyway. Elizabeth Otis was now handling Steinbeck's material, and she encouraged him to write more stories like "The Red Pony." Despite the demands made by caring for Olive, Steinbeck's creative energy was flowing at a high level. He spent every spare moment hunched over a ledger. The next piece he completed was "The Great Mountains," another story of Jody Tiflin, his family, and Billy Buck. There were other stories he wanted to write about Jody, but Steinbeck was also beginning in earnest the composition of another series of stories. These were concerned with the *paisanos* who lived in Tortilla Flat, outside Monterey. Steinbeck was convinced that he could take the material of the *paisanos'* lives and create from it a cycle of stories that would on the surface be humorous and entertaining, but which would carry deeper truths as well. Once more he thought of Malory and the *Morte d'Arthur*. Steinbeck's *paisano* stories would resonate with Malory's influence—in the easygoing, unambitious lives of the *paisanos*, Steinbeck found the material to create a modern Round Table. The quest of the *paisano* knights might be directed at the acquisition of bottles of wine rather than Holy Grails, but that made Steinbeck's series no less Arthurian. Elizabeth Otis was not enthusiastic about the *paisano* stories, but Steinbeck stuck with them through the summer and into the fall.

With two sets of related stories under way, Steinbeck also wrote some stories that stood by themselves. He did not feel up to the challenges of writing a novel, nor did the circumstances of the Steinbeck home permit the ongoing concentration that a novel required. Steinbeck began finding ways of writing short stories that were almost novels in themselves. His style grew simpler and simpler. He selected incidents that showed, in the space of a few pages and a brief series of carefully selected incidents, the frustrations and angers that dwelled within people whose lives were on the surface ordinary. One of these stories, "The Murder," dealt with a farmer who killed his wife's lover. Another, "The Chrysanthemums," captured perfectly in only a few thousand words the desperation of a farm wife who wanted some excitement in her life. When he finished one short story he began another. He had never worked so hard or so well.

In the fall he learned that Elizabeth Otis had placed "The Red Pony" and "The Great Mountains" with the *North American Review*, a prestigious but low-paying magazine that had a large audience. Although he received less than a hundred dollars for "The Red Pony" and barely fifty for "The Great Mountains" he and Carol indulged themselves with a great celebration. They needed the distraction and the hope that the sales offered. Olive was growing no better. John Ernst's health worsened each week. John Ernst was the county treasurer, and Steinbeck found himself spending some of his time at the treasurer's office, fulfilling John Ernst's political responsibilities. Steinbeck hated the work, but his own political awareness was increasing. Carol was employed as a secretary at the California Emergency Relief Association, one of the many state and federal agencies attempting to deal with the needs of people displaced by the deepening depression.

It was clear that the Great Depression was not simply going to go away. As the crisis worsened, the nation grew tense. Violence increased. In the summer of 1932 veterans of World War I had marched on Washington in hopes of securing a government bonus owed them. The government's response had been swift: mounted troops led by General Douglas MacArthur had drawn sabers and herded the destitute veterans like cattle through the streets of the capital. Later that year President Hoover was soundly defeated by Franklin Delano Roosevelt, who upon taking office in 1933 began boldly implementing dramatic changes and programs aimed at saving the economy and providing for the sick, the hungry, and the homeless.

Hoover was no longer president, but the communities named for him continued to grow. There was a Hooverville outside Salinas. It was called "Little Oklahoma" after its citizens, small farmers driven from their land by the failed economy and by the fierce windstorms that stripped the topsoil and flung it into the air in great, impenetrable clouds of dust. The Dust Bowl, as Oklahoma and its neighboring states were called, spread swiftly in area. Thousands of farm families loaded their belongings on what vehicles they could muster and set out for California in hopes of finding work as migrant laborers. The influx of migrants provided California's farmers with an inexhaustible pool of people who could be hired at wages far below subsistence levels. Whole families worked long hours in the lettuce fields and apple orchards for pennies a day. Not even Roosevelt, who had rallied the country with his example of courage and fearlessness, could provide a quick solution for the dispossessed and exploited.

Where the government failed, other organizations stepped in and tried to rally support. Among them was the Communist party, whose representatives urged the migrants to organize into labor unions. The collective strength of a union, organizers argued, could stand up to the exploitation of the migrants. A union could strike, forcing the farmers to raise their wages lest their crops rot in the fields and orchards. Violence erupted frequently between the farmers and the labor organizers. Communists and non-Communist organizers were lynched. As he read the newspaper accounts of such incidents, Steinbeck considered writing about a labor organizer. He thought that such a book, an autobiography of a fictional character, would provide a perfect format in which to explore further his thoughts and theories about group consciousness. The very idea of a union made a perfect metaphor for the group whose whole was greater than its individual parts. Steinbeck put the project aside when Elizabeth Otis informed him that the prospects for selling such a work were poor.

Even work he had completed did not sell well. *To a God Unknown* was published in November 1933, and the familiar pattern repeated itself once more. The novel received only a few reviews, none of them very favorable. Sales reports were even more gloomy: *To a God Unknown* would not come close to selling out its small first edition. Steinbeck was not discouraged. *To a God Unknown* had many good parts, but it seemed like something written by someone else. Joseph Wayne remained a striking character, and his relationship with the land was skillfully evoked. Yet Steinbeck had made his character too isolated. He saw that now and worked to correct the oversight in his new stories. Steinbeck was determined to write about people who were part of something larger than themselves. His concerns were reflected in "The Red Pony" and its sequels, which showed Jody Tiflin growing into the world of adults. The Tortilla Flat stories reflected Steinbeck's thinking as well. At the heart of the *paisano* stories was a character named Danny, the "King Arthur" of Tortilla Flat. For the *paisanos*, Tortilla Flat became a world itself.

The poor performance of *To a God Unknown* was offset the same month by the publication of "The Red Pony" in the *North American Review*'s November issue. The magazine's readers responded warmly to the long story of Jody Tiflin and his doomed colt. "The Great Mountains" was scheduled for the *North American Review's* December 1933 issue. In the coming months the magazine would buy other Steinbeck stories, among them "The Murder," "The White Quail," and a story about labor violence and Communists that Steinbeck called "The Raid." None of the sales paid very much, but publication brought Steinbeck's name to the attention of a far larger audience than he'd ever enjoyed.

Christmas 1933 was ghastly. Olive Steinbeck's faculties had disintegrated throughout the fall, and by the holiday season she was no longer capable of coherent thought. John Ernst had suffered some physical setbacks himself. His heart and eyes were growing weak, and the strain of watching his wife slowly lose her mind had exacted a large toll on his nerves. Still, John Ernst insisted that the house be decorated just as Olive had through every Christmas of their long marriage. Steinbeck and Carol went along with the charade, but it was a painful experience. Steinbeck knew that this would be the last Christmas for his mother. For a while Steinbeck feared that John Ernst might be dying as well.

On February 19, 1934, Olive Hamilton Steinbeck died. Her passing came as a relief after the long illness and decline. Once the funeral was behind them, Steinbeck, Carol, and John Ernst retired to the Pacific Grove cottage for a few weeks of rest. The months during which Olive lay dying had drained them of strength. Steinbeck and Carol felt tentative around each other— they had had very little privacy since the previous summer. In Pacific Grove, John Ernst rallied, and by the end of March was ready to move back to Salinas and resume his responsibilities as county treasurer. His son and daughter-in-law would not be going with him; John Ernst knew that it was time for the young couple to get on with their own lives. He arranged to take in a family of boarders who would help run the household as part of their rent.

Steinbeck and Carol celebrated their independence by accompanying Ed Ricketts on a specimen-collecting trip. A week of probing through tidal pools in search of octopus invigorated and rejuvenated them. Steinbeck was thinking of beginning a novel now that he had more free time. In conversations with Carol and Ricketts he began outlining the sort of novel he would like to try next. His short story "The Raid" had barely touched the surface of the problem of labor unrest. A long novel, though, would give him the room he needed in which not only to examine the political and personal roots of labor violence, but also to explore his increasingly complex theories of group consciousness. After the expedition was ended, he began making notes for the novel. Steinbeck and Carol divided their time between Pacific Grove and Salinas, where Carol went to work in the county treasurer's office, helping John Ernst catch up with the work left undone during Olive's illness.

While Carol worked, Steinbeck began researching labor unions. He approached this subject as he did his scientific investigations. Throughout the spring of 1934 he went on expeditions in search of firsthand information about migrant workers, about the Communists, about labor organizers, and about the farmers' rabid hatred of unions. His sheaf of notes grew thick with observations, reflections, bits of dialogue and local color. The Hoovervilles continued to increase in number and population, and Steinbeck visited them. The government was active in gathering the migrants into communities as well. Fearful that Communists might spark a revolution, federal camps and compounds were started, into which were shepherded the strikers and migrants. In such camps, the government reasoned, the hungry and homeless could be fed and given shelter. With the migrants' basic needs attended to, the revolutionary talk might dwindle and die away. Steinbeck discovered that the opposite was true—inside the fences that surrounded the government camps, thousands of migrants crowded together began to develop a distinctive group consciousness. The logic of the group will was taking over. By summer Steinbeck was nearly ready to start his new novel.

He wanted it to be a major effort. Steinbeck felt ready to embark upon a long novel, a book with a major theme. He had completed the *paisano* stories and called the book *Tortilla Flat*. Elizabeth Otis's lack of enthusiasm for the project was borne out by Robert Ballou, who rejected the book. Steinbeck's agents then showed *Tortilla Flat* to editors at Knopf, but it was turned down once more. His literary agent suggested that Steinbeck might want to consider doing another draft of the small book, but Steinbeck refused. He put *Tortilla Flat* out of his thoughts and began developing the characters and scenes for his novel. During the summer he worked on short stories about strikers and lynch mobs, exploring in advance some of the themes with which his novel would be concerned. In midsummer it was announced that "The Murder," which had appeared in the *North American Review*'s April 1934 issue, had been selected for inclusion in the next *O. Henry Prize Stories* volume, an annual collection of outstanding short fiction. The selection took some of the sting out of the failure of *Tortilla Flat* to find a publisher. Steinbeck hoped that his inclusion in the anthology would spark some increased public awareness of his work and its merits. In August he began his novel of labor unrest.

The book kept him busy through the fall. Nothing could distract him from his work. In November, John Ernst was defeated for re-election as county treasurer. The defeat was a blow to Steinbeck's father, who without work became more and more homebound, his contact with the outer world restricted to listening to the radio. At the same time, with John Ernst out of office, Steinbeck and Carol were freed from the hours of help they put in on the treasury records. They continued to visit Salinas occasionally, but they also felt more comfortable with leaving the area for long periods. Steinbeck did not forget how much he owed his father and hoped that John Ernst lived long enough to see him become not just a promising writer but a successful one.

Steinbeck's promise was being noted even as his books were remaindered by their publishers. Remaindered books are those taken out of inventory and sold in bulk to book dealers who in turn offered the volumes to their customers at large discounts. A bookseller in Chicago, Ben Abramson, was a great fan of Steinbeck's work and stocked up on remaindered copies of *The Pastures of Heaven*. He recommended the book to all of his customers. Abramson gave *The Pastures of Heaven* a particularly enthusiastic recommendation to Pascal Covici. A former Chicago bookseller himself, Covici had founded his own publishing house. After a few years of being based in Chicago, he had gone into partnership with Donald Friede, moving the operations of Covici-Friede to New York. Covici read *The Pastures of Heaven* immediately, and when he returned to New York, he contacted McIntosh & Otis. Steinbeck's agents sent Covici the manuscript of *Tortilla Flat*. The *paisano* stories appealed to the publisher from the very first paragraph:

"This is the story of Danny and of Danny's friends and of Danny's house. It is the story of how these three became one thing, so that in Tortilla Flat if you speak of Danny's house you do not mean a structure of wood flaked with old whitewash, overgrown with an ancient untrimmed rose of Castile. No, when you speak of Danny's house you are understood to mean a unit of which the parts are men, from which came sweetness and joy, philanthropy and, in the end, a mystic sorrow. For Danny's house was not unlike the Round Table, and Danny's friends were not unlike the knights of it. And this is the story of how that group came into being, of how it flourished and grew to be an organization beautiful and wise. This story deals with the adventuring of Danny's friends, with the good they did, with their thoughts and their endeavors. In the end, this story tells how the talisman was lost and how the group disintegrated."

Covici's excitement gathered as he read the subsequent pages. Steinbeck did not allow his determination to retell Malory's legends in modern terms get in the way of also telling a straightforward, very funny and touching story. The *paisanos* came alive on the page, their earthy and uncomplicated attitudes toward work, drinking, and sex providing a perfect antidote to the grimness of the depression. Covici informed McIntosh & Otis that he would like to publish *Tortilla Flat* and also to return Steinbeck's earlier books to print.

As Covici negotiated with his agents, Steinbeck pressed ahead with his new novel. He set his scene carefully, placing the action of the novel in an apple-growing valley in central California. Steinbeck's central character, a young man named Jim Nolan, joined the labor movement early in the book. The first section of the novel dealt with Jim's education in the tactics of organizing a strike against the apple growers. The strike, Jim learned quickly, was not expected to succeed. No strike could succeed; the labor organizers, understanding this, saw failed strikes as prelude for a larger, more violent revolution. The foredoomed battle against the farm owners gave Steinbeck his title. He called the novel *In Dubious Battle*.

Steinbeck leaned heavily upon dialogue to tell his story. For the most part his characters spoke crisply, their language and attitudes passionate and angry. Midway through the book, though, Steinbeck used a character named Doc Burton to give full voice to his own theories:

"'When you cut your finger, and streptococci get in the wound, there's a swelling and a soreness. That swelling is the fight your body puts up, the pain is the battle. You can't tell which one is going to win, but the wound is the first battleground. If the cells lose the first fight the streptococci invade, and the fight goes on up the arm. Mac, these little strikes are like the infection. Something had got into the men; a little fever had started and the lymphatic glands are shooting in reinforcements. I want to see, so I go to the seat of the wound.'"

"'You figure the strike is a wound?'"

"'Yes. Group-men are always getting some kind of infection. This seems to be a bad one. I want to *see*, Mac. I want to watch these group-men, for they seem to me to be a new individual, not at all like single men. A man in a group isn't himself at all, he's a cell in an organism that isn't like him any more than the cells in your body are like you. I want to watch the group and see what it's like. People have said, "mobs are crazy, you can't tell what they'll do." Why don't people look at mobs not as men but as mobs? A mob nearly always seems to act reasonably, for a mob.' "

As 1934 drew to a close, Steinbeck saw the end of *In Dubious Battle* approaching. He wrote furiously, building the novel's pace and tension until the final confrontation, in which Jim Nolan, a group-man, is killed. Jim's death is like the death of a cell: group-man will go on. Steinbeck completed the novel in February 1935. Despite Covici-Friede's interest in his work, Steinbeck did not have great hopes for *In Dubious Battle*. The novel was as true as he could make it, both in its presentation of the physical details of migrant workers, strikers, and farmers, and also in its representation of the philosophy Steinbeck was developing. He knew, however, that the novel hewed to no party line, other than Steinbeck's own conclusions. He had written the kind of novel that would be criticized by capitalists and Communists alike. When he mailed the manuscript to his agents, he anticipated their criticism of *In Dubious Battle*'s structure and informed McIntosh & Otis that the book could not be changed. Steinbeck knew that the book made no neat patterns, that all of its loose ends were not tied up, that the book simply stopped, rather than achieving a dramatic, satisfying climax. That had been his intention. Reality provided no simple resolutions, and Steinbeck was unwilling to create them for his fiction. He informed McIntosh & Otis that he was not after the creation of perfect works of art. Rather, Steinbeck wanted to write novels that were as formless and unstructured as life itself. He was aware that such an approach would cause difficulty with literary critics, but he would not cut his work to suit critical taste.

The same month he finished *In Dubious Battle*, Steinbeck signed the contracts for publication of *Tortilla Flat*. Covici-Friede, like all of the other publishers Steinbeck had dealt with, was in poor financial health. Nevertheless, Covici planned a handsome edition for the *paisano* stories and commissioned a series of line drawings as illustrations. McIntosh & Otis forwarded the manuscript of *In Dubious Battle* to Covici-Friede. Covici himself was out of New York when Steinbeck's novel arrived, and the book was given to one of the publisher's junior editors, a man of pronounced Communist sympathies. The editor read *In Dubious Battle* quickly and just as quickly rejected the novel. In his letter of rejection he pointed out all the errors in Communist dogma that Steinbeck had made, and implied that the novel failed to live up to its social—and socialist—responsibilities. Steinbeck's predictions were proved accurate before the novel was published.

When Covici returned to New York and learned what had happened, he became livid. Covici fired the editor immediately and set to work patching up his relationship with Steinbeck. McIntosh & Otis had put *In Dubious Battle* back on the market and had already found several publishers, Random House, Knopf, and Bobbs-Merrill among them, quite interested in adding the novel of labor unrest to their lists. Steinbeck, angry at the ideological rejection of his novel, nonetheless agreed to return the book to Covici-Friede. Once the misunderstanding had been settled, Covici got to work preparing for the spring publication of *Tortilla Flat*.

Steinbeck was exhausted from months of work on *In Dubious Battle*. He was further distracted by his father's physical collapse. John Ernst was suffering from a series of cerebral accidents that caused leakage of blood in his brain. He was being nursed now by his daughter Esther. There was no doubt that John Ernst was dying, and the prospect of his father's death left Steinbeck depressed. There were hints that *Tortilla Flat* would do well when it appeared, and Steinbeck was aware that the new book, like all his books, could not have been written without his father's support and encouragement. Their disagreement over college seemed distant and insignificant. Once it had become clear that Steinbeck not only wanted to be a writer, but that he could write books that would be published, he found no greater champion than his father. John Ernst had called on bookstores and libraries, carrying copies of his son's work. The failure of *Cup of Gold, The Pastures of Heaven,* and *To a God Unknown* to attract large audiences seemed to annoy John Ernst far more than it annoyed Steinbeck himself. Not long before his collapse, John Ernst had told Steinbeck that he had been frustrated all of his life, that he had never been able to pursue the interests that most appealed to him. From that frustration had come the indulgence and support that enabled Steinbeck to remain committed to his own dreams. John Ernst Steinbeck died on May 23, 1935. Five days later *Tortilla Flat* was published and became an instant success.

The lively little book about the *paisanos* struck a sympathetic chord with the reading public. For the first time in his career Steinbeck enjoyed good reviews, many of which actually seemed aware of the Arthurian philosophy that underlay Steinbeck's stories. Whether or not the public was attentive to Steinbeck's philosophy was another matter, but there was no doubt that American readers enjoyed *Tortilla Flat* immensely. By late summer the book was climbing onto some best-seller lists, and Steinbeck and Carol for the first time faced the prospect of having enough money to live comfortably.

The success was bittersweet. John Ernst had left his son one final subsidy. The estate provided a few thousand dollars for Steinbeck and Carol, enough for them to live quietly for a couple of years while Steinbeck worked on new books. As the summer progressed and the sales of *Tortilla Flat* soared, it became clear that the book might earn as much money as Steinbeck had inherited. In August, Covici traveled to the West Coast where he presented Steinbeck with his first royalty payment, a check for several hundred dollars. Covici and Steinbeck enjoyed each other's company, and Steinbeck revealed that now, with his finances in good shape, he was considering a rewrite of *In*

Dubious Battle. Covici dissuaded him. They needed to follow the success of *Tortilla Flat* as quickly as possible. *In Dubious Battle* would be published by Covici-Friede in January 1936. Covici felt certain the book would consolidate Steinbeck's success.

More than Steinbeck's finances were changing. He found himself becoming a celebrity, and it was a position he loathed. He refused to give personal interviews and flew into a rage at a journalist who printed the color of his eyes. *Tortilla Flat* spawned some local controversy as well. The Monterey Chamber of Commerce was angered by the book's portrayal of *paisanos*, whom many more respectable citizens thought of as "trash." Steinbeck and Carol were able to laugh at the chamber's displeasure; Carol particularly was not concerned with annoying her old employer. The chamber feared that the novel would hurt the area's tourist business, but the opposite was true. By fall a steady stream of visitors to Monterey included a look at the real Tortilla Flat on their itineraries. Too many of them also wanted a glimpse of John Steinbeck himself. Steinbeck hated being the focus of so much attention. It interfered with his work. He and Carol decided to travel to Mexico for several months' rejuvenation.

They stayed for a while in Mexico City. In October a telegram from McIntosh & Otis reached them there. Paramount studios had purchased the motion picture rights to *Tortilla Flat* for $4,000. Steinbeck's depression deepened. He did not want to be considered a popular writer, and the prospect of becoming wealthy as a result of his work frightened him. Through all the years of poverty he had remained dedicated to writing only what he wanted to write. If those works failed to live up to the expectations of publishers or the public, at least Steinbeck could be satisfied that he had maintained his own integrity. Now that he was building an audience he worried that the books he planned might be compromised in hopes of repeating the success of *Tortilla Flat*. At the same time he was aware that he had written nothing of importance since completing *In Dubious Battle* early in the year. He wondered if he would ever write anything worthwhile again.

Late in the year Steinbeck and Carol left Mexico and traveled to New York. Covici was already generating publicity for the forthcoming edition of *In Dubious Battle*. Covici-Friede had also brought *The Pastures of Heaven* and *To a God Unknown* back into print and were planning a new edition of *Cup of Gold*. Steinbeck and Carol spent Christmas 1935 in Pacific Grove. They learned that *Tortilla Flat* had been selected by the Commonwealth Club of California as the state's best novel of 1935. In keeping with his abhorrence of publicity and public appearances, Steinbeck would not attend the presentation of the Club's Gold Medal. He and Carol began talking of buying a more secluded property where they could get away from the gathering attention. Steinbeck was eager to get back to work.

Shortly after the first of the year his plans were interrupted by the publication of *In Dubious Battle*. The critical reception surprised Steinbeck with its gentleness. Reviewers on both the right and the left of the political spectrum argued that Steinbeck was working for their side. Only a very few reviewers, among them Mary McCarthy, who would forge a career as a political novelist and essayist herself, openly attacked the novel. Such attacks pilloried Steinbeck for misrepresenting—or misunderstanding—the nature of American communism and the American labor movement. Steinbeck felt that the misunderstanding belonged to the critics. The politics of *In Dubious Battle* were far less important than the novel's philosophy. The few critics that noticed the group-man philosophy disparaged it as sophomoric or less than fully thought-out.

Steinbeck and Carol bought two acres of land near Los Gatos in Santa Clara County, midway to the north between Monterey and San Francisco. They began building a house for their small ranch. Steinbeck worked hard on the grounds, building flower beds, transplanting shrubbery, planning a vegetable garden. As he labored outside, his mind was on the novel. He had some trouble finding the right way to start the book. Steinbeck wanted to write a simpler novel than *In Dubious Battle*, or at least one whose language and structure were simpler. He told his friends that the new book would be written with such a carefullly restricted vocabulary that a child could read it. The story took place in a familiar setting, the Salinas Valley. It dealt with the friendship of two wandering farm workers, a small man named George and a mentally deficient giant of a man named Lennie. Steinbeck had been pleased with the objectivity he brought to *In Dubious Battle*, but he wanted to go even further with "Something That Happened," as he called his new story. He wanted to disappear from the page as much as possible.

By spring he was no longer thinking of "Something That Happened" as a formal novel at all. He was trying to take his work in a direction that was experimental and risky. This new book would fall somewhere between being a novel and being a play. Theater was already much on his thoughts. The dramatic rights for *In Dubious Battle* had been sold, and the producers commissioned a writer named John O'Hara to talk with Steinbeck about the adaptation. O'Hara was establishing himself as a promising novelist as well, and he and Steinbeck became friends. Steinbeck listened to O'Hara's thoughts about theater and to O'Hara's encouragement that he try writing a play himself. Steinbeck stuck with the strategy he'd adopted for "Something That Happened." He wanted to combine the best virtues of both forms, and from that combination create something new.

His twin jobs of writing and grounds keeping kept Steinbeck occupied throughout the spring and summer. Carol spent her time making their small new home comfortable, buoying Steinbeck's spirits as much as she could. The late reviews for *In Dubious Battle* were less favorable than had been the initial notices. Steinbeck's difficulties with "Something That Happened" seemed at times insoluble. For his new approach to the novel to be effective, Steinbeck had to pare his prose down as far as was possible. Most of the story must be told in dialogue, with only enough stage setting and narrative to give the piece a sense of completeness. There was no room in this new book for reflective passages or lengthy descriptions. The task was as hard as any writer could set himself or herself, and more than once Steinbeck did not feel up to it. He would not give up. Every day he went to his ledger and waited, drawing on all the willpower he could muster. Some days it took hours for him to get started, but he never left his desk until some of the book was done. Each time he thought he had finished the book he found himself unsatisfied and started again. At one point a pet dog chewed up weeks of work. Often Steinbeck felt like a cheat, his doubts about his abilities and the value of the work he'd already done deepening.

Finally the story caught fire. Steinbeck had made so many attempts at "Something That Happened" that when the pace of creation picked up, he raced through a complete draft in less than two months. It was as though he'd spent the spring learning how to write the story he wanted to write. By the end of summer it was done. The story of George and Lennie's bond, and the tragedy that destroys that bond, was thirty thousand words long. It was a powerful story that needed a stronger title than the too-objective "Something That Happened." He called the new novel *Of Mice and Men*.

As always, Steinbeck was uncertain whether his work had any value. His literary agents and Pascal Covici were impressed with the novel, although they may have wished for a longer book. But the story itself was masterful and would appeal to anyone who could read. All were confident that this book, like the two that preceded it, would be a success. For his part, Steinbeck was pleased that *Tortilla Flat* and *In Dubious Battle* had made some money for his agents, who had displayed such faith in his promise. Steinbeck was also increasingly comfortable with "Pat" Covici, who took such care to publish Steinbeck as an important young author. During the summer Covici had even brought out two limited editions of individual Steinbeck stories. These were handsomely made little books for collectors. Covici also used the small books to promote Steinbeck's career. Steinbeck worried that Covici might be too hopeful about the commercial prospects for *Of Mice and Men.* It was not the sort of book, Steinbeck felt, that would have a large success.

With the completed novel in New York, Steinbeck accepted a newspaper commission that had been offered by the *San Francisco News.* Unrest between the farmers and the migrant laborers was growing. The Dust Bowl was driving tens of thousands from Oklahoma, Texas, Arkansas. Others were being displaced by bankruptcy or by the tractor and other tools of mechanized farming that the small farmer could not compete with. The heart of the nation was dying, and many of its people worked their way to California where they hoped to follow the harvests from valley to valley, from crop to crop. Because of the reputation for understanding farm and labor problems that he'd acquired as a result of *In Dubious Battle,* Steinbeck seemed to the *News* to be the perfect journalist for their assignment. He was to examine the state of conditions in the migrant workers' camps. Only a very few of the camps were operated by the government. Others were little more than gatherings of migrants, and still others were located on the farms themselves and were operated by the farmers. Steinbeck set out to investigate the problem.

At his first stop, the Gridley Migrant Camp in Sacramento, Steinbeck discovered that the farmers considered him to be part of the problem. He learned, in fact, that his life might be in danger. California's farmers saw Steinbeck as more dangerous than the labor organizers he'd written about. Steinbeck had a larger audience, and his words carried more weight. In Sacramento, Steinbeck was warned that the farmers had begun circulating his photograph among their employees and associates. There was a possibility that violent action would be taken against him. The process of law was breaking down. The larger farmers were illegally deputizing employees, creating private police forces. There had been lynchings and other incidents of vigilante violence. No one could guarantee Steinbeck's safety if he continued his tour of the migrant camps.

Steinbeck did not need guarantees. He would not be frightened away by the farmers' threats. He knew now that the picture he'd painted in *In Dubious Battle* was, for all its realism and brutality, too mild. He'd been too preoccupied with the ideas he wanted to present to perceive fully that ideas were alien to the migrant situation in California. The conditions were too grim. The government camps were barely acceptable—at least they provided water, medicine, toilet facilities, and a place for migrants to pitch their tents. But there were fewer than ten government camps, and they could only accommodate a small portion of the migrants. Steinbeck began investigating the conditions faced by those not fortunate enough to find space in a government camp.

Many of the migrants simply built squatter communities on the banks of irrigation ditches, fashioning their shelter from whatever scraps they could scrounge. Were it not for the clusters of people huddling together, the squatters' camps could have been mistaken for trash dumps. At least the migrants living in government camps retained some of their dignity. In a squatters' camp there was no dignity. A newly homeless squatter might try for a while to keep standards alive, sending raggedly clothed children off to school, digging a toilet ditch beside the scraps of cardboard that served as a family's walls and roof. Those who had been on the road longer held out no pretense of civilization— Steinbeck saw families sleeping in the midst of their own waste, surrounded by clouds of flies. Drinking water was filthy, bathing an impossibility, disease rampant. When children died, their bodies were collected by the local coroner. The faces of the living were lined with terror. Their greatest fear was starvation, but Steinbeck learned that sometimes the vigilantes attacked the squatters, burning their cardboard and rags. The tactics were aimed at keeping the migrants from organizing.

Many of the larger farms operated their own migrant camps. In a farm-run camp, the migrants were rented a shack with no running water or electricity, no beds or bedding. The streets of farm camps were patrolled by farm deputies. The deputies were armed, and they would use their guns against organizers. By the time the migrants paid rent for their one-room shack and purchased water and food from the farmers, they had nothing left. Wages were only a few cents an hour. Children began working the fields as soon as they could. No one dared speak out against the conditions. There was always a company worker nearby who could overhear and who would evict a whole family over the slightest complaint. The deputies knew what the farmers knew—there were plenty of other homeless families to take the places of any troublemakers who were kicked out.

Steinbeck was profoundly shaken by what he saw and heard. He became friends with Thomas Collins, a government camp administrator in Bakersfield, California. Collins kept comprehensive records of the migrant situation and worked to make statistical portraits out of the information he collected. Like Steinbeck, Collins was fascinated with group psychology, and he and Steinbeck passed many hours discussing the roots of mob violence and the vigilante impulse. For a time they discussed writing a book that would be based in part on the records Collins kept. In the statistics there was a portrait of solid American citizens reduced to stealing food, to easy infection and quick death, to wallowing in filth and despair. Covici advised against the book when Steinbeck wrote to suggest it. Steinbeck concentrated on turning his heartbreaking observations into a series of strong newspaper articles.

He called his series "The Harvest Gypsies" and completed the pieces in early fall. The *San Francisco News* declined to run them immediately, telling Steinbeck that they feared his work would stir up even more violence. The rejection was different only in degree from those he'd received as a young man. Newspapers, Steinbeck was reminded, sometimes feared printing the truth because the truth might upset their advertisers and readers. Steinbeck was furious. He'd worked hard on "The Harvest Gypsies," creating an accurate portrait of the degradation and misery that the migrants suffered. It was a portrait that would not let him go. Coupled with his conversations with Collins, his observations formed the basis of a new vision of group-man, of the collective will. Steinbeck had learned that even in the most dehumanizing of conditions, the migrants struggled to retain what dignity and compassion they could. If he could not get a newspaper to print his pieces, then he could transform his experiences and observations into fiction, for which he felt certain there was a market. The *News* relented at last and published "The Harvest Gypsies" during the week of October 5 through 12, 1936.

Steinbeck was already at work again, trying to give some shape to his experiences among the migrants. As a focus for his novel, he fashioned a vigilante confrontation. He gave the book a working title, "L'Affaire Lettuceberg," but could not make the narrative come to satisfactory life. He was ready to make a major effort and wanted the ambitious new novel to be a work of art as well as a piece of damning social commentary. He and Carol calculated late in 1936 that they would have enough money to get through two years of writing if they lived carefully. The new book, Steinbeck thought, would be worth the sacrifice. What he did not know was that across the country, in New York, word was beginning to spread that John Steinbeck had written a masterpiece called *Of Mice and Men*. As publication day approached, it became clear that the book would be successful beyond anyone's hopes and that Steinbeck's life would never be the same again.

SIX

THE GRAPES OF WRATH

By February 1937, there seemed to Steinbeck a good chance that he and Carol would become wealthy as a result of *Of Mice and Men*. The novel had been selected by the Book-of-the-Month Club, a sign that it would appeal to large numbers of readers. Covici had done a good job of promoting the book before publication as well. At first glance the story seemed too slight to be an important piece of fiction, but Covici had put out the word that John Steinbeck had written a masterpiece of simplicity. In a small frame, Steinbeck told a large story. That story's background—economic conditions, the life of the migrant, farming, the land itself—was implied by Steinbeck in a handful of paragraphs scattered through the book like stage directions. Everything else was in the foreground of the novel, all dialogue and movement. Interest in the dramatic rights to *Of Mice and Men* began to mount before the book was published. Covici increased the size of the first printing and still had to return to press quickly to print enough copies to meet demand. *Of Mice and Men* was published in March, and within its first few weeks sold more than a hundred thousand copies. Dramatic rights were acquired for a large sum. The play was set to open in the fall, under the supervision of George S. Kaufman, perhaps the brightest name in American theater at the time.

Steinbeck was stunned. He claimed that he could not comprehend wealth beyond the few dollars he might have in his pockets at any given time. He feared that money would disrupt his life, perhaps beyond repair. Along with the money came increasing celebrity. Already he was being recognized on the streets of San Francisco. The attention sickened him. His mail increased daily; there was no hope of answering it all. The changes in his life affected his work. "L'Affaire Lettuceberg" was giving Steinbeck great difficulty. He could not bring the book under control. Steinbeck wanted to write movingly about the plight of the migrants, a big book with a big theme. Instead, he found himself producing a short satire, bitter and sophomoric. Finally he put the manuscript aside. Wealth might cause problems, but at least he could now afford to indulge his love of travel. He could get away from his desk. In April, Steinbeck and Carol sailed to New York on board a freighter.

The attention Steinbeck had begun to attract in San Francisco was nothing compared to the reception he found in New York. John Steinbeck was a famous man. He was no star on the order of a motion picture actress or a baseball player, but as a successful novelist Steinbeck was beset with requests for autographs, photographs, interviews. He did not tolerate the requests with good grace. Steinbeck carried a bottle of liquor to a press conference and during the questioning drank openly from it. He wanted to show his contempt for the press but ended up only creating more notoriety for himself. Carol was drinking heavily as well. They pursued what distraction they could with a New York shopping spree, but after two and a half weeks the Steinbecks had had their fill of the city. They were, in fact, planning to leave the country altogether. In May, Steinbeck and Carol boarded the SS *Drottningholm*, bound for Scandinavia.

Sea voyages always refreshed Steinbeck. In Scandinavia he encountered an attitude toward his work that was equally rejuvenating. Steinbeck met many people who knew his name, but unlike Americans they also knew his books. It was the books that people wanted to talk about, not how much money their author earned or how much he drank or what his marriage was like. Steinbeck began regaining some perspective about his work and its importance. He felt a renewed interest in ideas and decided to visit the Soviet Union. Two decades had passed since the Russian Revolution that brought Communists to power. Steinbeck wanted to see how the Soviet government and the Russian people might exemplify his theories about group-man and the collective society. Visiting Moscow and Leningrad in July, Steinbeck discovered that economic conditions in the Soviet Union were even more frightful than those in the United States. Nor had the Soviet government achieved the creation of anything but a state in which the individual spirit—of which group spirit must be composed—was extinguished wherever it appeared. Without individuality, the collective has no soul, Steinbeck realized. He made up his mind that he would someday visit the Soviet Union again, for a longer period of time, and more diligently pursue his initial insights. By late summer Steinbeck and Carol were back in New York.

The excitement surrounding Steinbeck had not abated. *Of Mice and Men* was still selling well. The dramatic version was progressing quickly under Kaufman's control. There was also interest in the dramatic rights to *Tortilla Flat*. While he was overseas, Steinbeck had had another book published. Covici had been after him for some time to continue the story of the Tiflin family begun in "The Red Pony." Steinbeck had written a third story in the series before he left California, but he had urged Covici to wait until a fourth story was written before publishing the series in a single volume. Covici had other plans. With Steinbeck's grudging permission, the publisher took the three Tiflin family stories and produced a slim, beautifully designed and manufactured book for collectors. The book was priced at ten dollars, twice the price of the more than one thousand page *Gone With the Wind*. Nevertheless, *The Red Pony* in its first, expensive book incarnation sold out its entire edition. Collectors wanted to own every item that Steinbeck published. Steinbeck was disgusted.

He had tried to get started on "L'Affaire Lettuceberg" on the voyage back from Scandinavia. The book went no better than it had in California. For a time after his return Steinbeck retired to George S. Kaufman's farm to work with Kaufman on adapting *Of Mice and Men* for the stage. Steinbeck hated the process: it was too much like being part of a committee. Unlike writing novels where on the page he could do whatever he wished, Steinbeck discovered that the playwright must take any number of technical considerations into account. Where would the actors stand when they delivered his speeches? How would the set be lighted to best display Steinbeck's truths? How might the pace of certain scenes be picked up to better serve not only dramatic tension but also audience interest? In the onslaught of such questions and considerations, Steinbeck worried that the truth of his story might be lost completely. Finally he decided to leave the adaptation in the hands of Kaufman and other theatrical professionals. Over their protest he bought a car and set out to drive across the country. Stopping only in Chicago to visit his uncle, Joseph Hamilton—so proud now of the nephew who had once turned down an advertising career in order to be free to write books—Steinbeck set himself a steady pace. He was eager to be back at his small place near Los Gatos.

Once he got there in early fall, Steinbeck discovered that the lovely private spot had lost its isolation as a result of its owner's new fame. Tourists, autographs seekers, Hollywood producers, and people who never read books but enjoyed meeting authors—all paraded past his home in growing numbers. The daily mail had become a deluge of requests for money and advice. Young writers wrote to enlist Steinbeck's help in getting published. His success was also affecting Steinbeck's relationship with some of his oldest friends. He felt estranged from people he had known and been close to throughout his adult life. Some of the members of the writing group from his Stanford days now were openly jealous of Steinbeck and his achievements. He was accused of selling out his talent and ideals. It was an accusation that particularly stung Steinbeck; success was cutting him off from his own past.

No less painful was the fact that he was just as cut off from his own work. He began his novel of vigilante violence once more from the beginning, but broke off after only a little work. Steinbeck wanted to do more firsthand research. On his cross-country drive he had seen mile after mile of roadway along whose sides camped the destitute and the homeless. Steinbeck got in touch with Tom Collins again to arrange a new tour of migrant camps. For a time Steinbeck planned to trace the route of migration all the way back to Oklahoma. His novel would be about "Okies," as the migrants were derisively called. At the time it was a term as hateful as "nigger" or "kike." Steinbeck did not make the complete journey to Oklahoma, but he did visit several camps and stopped to speak with people fighting for survival at roadside. Steinbeck took it all in, seeking ways to turn the mass migration into the background of his book. He wanted to focus upon the conflict between successful large farmers and the migrants they exploited and terrorized. He tried as much as he was able to share the migrants' fears and hopes. Steinbeck did not want his new success to interfere with a truthful telling of what he saw. By November he was back in Los Gatos, ready to resume the writing of novels.

There was one more large interruption. *Of Mice and Men* was set to open at Broadway's Music Box Theater on November 23. Steinbeck was under some pressure from George S. Kaufman and others to return to New York for opening night. Steinbeck refused to make the journey. Kaufman's displeasure offended and annoyed Steinbeck, who angrily wrote his agents that he would not travel all the way across the United States to witness the resurrection of Jesus Christ. *Of Mice and Men*, even without its creator present, opened very successfully to good reviews. The play was a hit with audiences from the moment the first curtain rose. During the premiere, Pat Covici sent Steinbeck a telegram after every act. Following the final curtain call, his agents telephoned Steinbeck and told him over a tenuous cross-country connection that *Of Mice and Men* promised to be as large a smash on stage as it had proved in the bookstores. Even Steinbeck, whose recalcitrance had ruffled so many feathers during the development of the play, admitted to suffering from transcontinental stage fright on opening night. By way of celebrating this latest success, Steinbeck purchased his very first brand-new typewriter. He used the machine to write letters, taking delight as always in the functioning of a well-made piece of machinery. Fiction, though, required one of his familiar ledgers. As though certain the new novel would require little revision, Steinbeck worked in ink rather than pencil.

He would dip the pen in blood, if he could. Where the vigilante novel had been satirical in the "L'Affaire Lettuceberg" draft, the book now became ugly. Steinbeck boasted of his new work's nastiness and expressed a regret that he could not make the story nastier still. His characters would be a gallery of grotesques, his incidents as brutal and graphic as he could make them. The events of the past year and the pressures of success had built up in him. Steinbeck was going to hit back with a frightful book. He worked hard at it through the early months of winter and on into the new year. He was not even distracted by the New York premiere of the dramatic version of *Tortilla Flat*. *Of Mice and Men* had been transformed into a fine, strong play that was a genuine contribution to American theater. *Tortilla Flat* had not even been turned into a good entertainment. It was a show, not a play, and it was a bad show. Carol traveled East early in January to be present on *Tortilla Flat*'s opening night. The play was poorly written and turned Steinbeck's life-loving *paisanos* into tawdry drunks. Poorly acted and incompetently directed, *Tortilla Flat* was an embarrassment that opened and closed in less than a week. On the other hand, *Of Mice and Men* was entering its third month of capacity houses. Kaufman's adaptation was generating substantial revenues. Steinbeck received large checks virtually every week.

Writing a novel whose purpose was to disgust was the hardest work Steinbeck had undertaken. The anger he had to rouse as he sat to his ledger each morning carried over into the hours after he stopped working. He and his wife were fighting more frequently. Carol's trip to New York had cheered her for a while, but as winter deepened and Steinbeck's involvement with the novel became complete, she grew unhappy. The Los Gatos house and grounds on which they had both worked so hard now seemed cramped and constrictive. Carol began looking for another, larger piece of property where they could build a more suitable home. Heavy, constant rains made February even more bleak.

The rains flooded California's rivers. Tens of thousands of migrants tried to survive days mired in mud. No fruits or vegetables remained to be found by scavengers. Ragged clothing hung sodden against clammy skin. No cardboard home could stand up to the rains. Starvation, the constant specter on the edge of the migrant worker's life, now became a reality. Hit hardest, as always, were the children. Whole families were dying, the youngest first. Government aid moved slowly at best. The corporate farmers did nothing to alleviate a situation that was to their best interest—a large, demoralized work force meant that it was easy to fill the fields during harvest and planting times. *Life* magazine wanted coverage of the tragedy and commissioned Steinbeck to accompany a photographer on a tour of the flooded areas. He was glad to have the chance to turn the angry themes of his novel into an angry piece of journalism. He wrote the article for *Life* quickly, telling of the euphemism "malnutrition" on the death certificates of children who had starved. Steinbeck informed his audience of the ease with which a doctor could be summoned to lie on a death certificate, the impossibility of finding a physician who would treat an illness. The article was as blunt as he could make it.

It was too blunt for *Life's* editors. They rejected the piece when Steinbeck was unwilling to soften the language in which he described the dying migrants, the government's failure, the corporations' greed and indifference. Nor would California newspapers publish the piece, which Steinbeck called "Starvation Under the Orange Trees." Only after months of being turned down by magazines and newspapers was Steinbeck able to place the piece. It appeared in a small Monterey paper but attracted larger attention. California's Simon J. Lubin Society—named for one of the state's first advocates of the rights of migrant farm laborers—wanted to reprint Steinbeck's "Harvest Gypsies" articles in pamphlet form. The pamphlet would be called *Their Blood Is Strong.* Steinbeck contributed "Starvation Under the Orange Trees," slightly revised to make it a suitable epilogue to his earlier pieces. He hoped the pamphlet would arouse the public.

Steinbeck was trying to reach the same end with his novel. By the first of May he was done with the book's new draft. It was a short novel of about twice the size of *Of Mice and Men.* Covici was eager to get the manuscript, planning to bring it out quickly. His publishing firm was in financial difficulty, despite the income produced by Steinbeck's work, and Covici needed another successful book as soon as possible. Steinbeck surprised Covici by declining to submit the manuscript as it stood. The book was too ugly, too grotesque. It had not accomplished what Steinbeck wanted and was successful neither as fiction nor as political argument. He would have to try again. A bright note came late in the month when *Of Mice and Men* won the New York Drama Critics Circle Award, being named the best American play of the preceding year. Covici planned a large collection of Steinbeck short stories, hoping to capitalize at least a bit on his prize author's continued success and acclaim.

Steinbeck spent most of May getting ready to approach his novel once more. He was spending a good amount of time in Monterey with Ed Ricketts. Pacific Biological Laboratories had encountered financial difficulties, from which it was rescued when Steinbeck bought into the company and quietly became Ricketts's partner. They talked of expanding the firm's operations, of mounting expeditions in search of scientific knowledge and marine specimens. Steinbeck and Ricketts continued their philosophical discussions. Steinbeck wanted his next attempt at a novel based upon the migrant experience to be philosophical in tone, where the previous versions had been satirical and brutal in turn. He put aside the idea of structuring the novel around an episode of vigilante violence. Steinbeck needed a larger form for the story he now wanted to tell. Steinbeck was going to write an American epic. He would tell the story of a long and arduous trek—a quest—embarked upon by a family, the Joads, who were bereft of anything other than hope of a promised land at journey's end.

By early summer he was well into the new draft, a bit frightened by the ease with which the book was appearing on the pages of his ledger. Nothing could break his concentration, although there were plenty of distractions. Carol was negotiating for a fifty-acre tract near Los Gatos—she wanted to build a new house where she and Steinbeck might recover some of their lost privacy. Word came from New York that Pat Covici had gone bankrupt. Works Covici had under contract—including, of course, Steinbeck's—were seized by a printer as collateral against Covici's debts; other creditors froze money meant for royalty payments. Steinbeck held out hope for Covici to reach an accommodation with his creditors but worried about who would publish his new book. Once it was clear that Steinbeck's publisher had gone under, McIntosh & Otis began receiving letters of inquiry from most of America's publishing houses. Each was eager to add Steinbeck's name to its lists, although Steinbeck did not like the idea of starting all over again with a new publisher.

Steinbeck's social circle was widening as well: during the summer he became close with Charles Chaplin. Steinbeck was seeing more and more people who were wealthy, powerful, influential. As one of America's best-selling young novelists, Steinbeck found that those same words applied to him. As if all the other demands and requests upon his time were not enough, Steinbeck found himself caring for Carol during an extended bout with strep throat and a subsequent tonsillectomy.

Yet the book was coming too quickly and too well to be stopped. By August he had written a hundred thousand words and estimated that he was halfway through his story. He had known all summer that this would be a long book and that it would sprawl out in many directions, against all accepted ideas of proper novelistic form and structure. Steinbeck was breaking the rules once more. The centerpiece of the book was the story of the Joads, their journey to California, their discovery of the true nature of the promised land. Narrative and characters came together almost perfectly. But Steinbeck was not restricting himself to narrative. He interleaved his narrative chapters with shorter, more impressionistic chapters. In these sections Steinbeck used an astonishing range of voices and techniques. Some of the passages read as though they were sociological reports, others as though transcriptions of people's innermost thoughts, a technique known as stream of consciousness. In some of the short interchapters Steinbeck seemed to come directly on stage, lecturing the reader. In others he was completely absent, a dispassionate narrator making a scientific report.

The novel was able to support such a variety of techniques because its central story was so strong. Steinbeck knew the Joads as well as he knew himself. He had met families like the Joads, had talked with them as they sought escape from the incessant rain and mud, had comforted them as they spoke of the children they had lost, had tried to encourage them as they shivered in fear of their own future. He was putting all of this on the page

now. He created characters some of whose aspects were as
grotesque or animalistic as any he'd ever created. But there was
also a great deal of love in the book, and a great deal of insight.
Tom Joad, back from prison in time to find his family setting out
from a home that they had lost, gave the novel a strong central
character. Ma Joad provided the novel with an emotional heart.
Tom's sister, Rose of Sharon, swelling with new life, riding across
country in the back of a truck trying only to care for the baby
within her served Steinbeck well both as a character and also as a
symbol of the renewal of the human spirit and the human race.
Steinbeck was putting everything he had in this novel. He would
build his story to a series of peaks and, after each one, insert an
interchapter in which he addressed in more general terms the
Joads' problems, which were also the world's problems:

"One man, one family driven from the land; this rusty car
creaking along the highway to the west. I lost my land, a single
tractor took my land. I am alone and I am bewildered. And in
the night one family camps in a ditch and another family pulls in
and the tents come out. The two men squat on their hams and
the women and children listen. Here is the node, you who hate
change and fear revolution. Keep these two squatting men apart;
make them hate, fear, suspect each other. Here is the anlage of
the thing you fear. This is the zygote. For here 'I lost my land' is
changed; a cell is split and from its splitting grows the thing you
hate—'We lost *our* land.' The danger is here, for two men are
not as lonely and perplexed as one. And from this first 'we' there
grows a still more dangerous thing: 'I have a little food' plus 'I
have none.' If from this problem the sum is 'We have a little
food,' the thing is on its way, the movement has direction. Only a
little multiplication now, and this land, this tractor are ours. The
two men squatting in a ditch, the little fire, the sidemeat stewing
in a single pot, the silent, stone-eyed women; behind, the children listening with their souls to words their minds do not
understand. The night draws down. The baby has a cold. Here,

take this blanket. It's wool. It was my mother's blanket—take it for the baby. This is the thing to bomb. This is the beginning—from 'I' to 'we.'

"If you who own the things people must have could understand this, you might preserve yourself. If you could separate causes from results, if you could know that Paine, Marx, Jefferson, Lenin, were results, not causes, you might survive. But that you cannot know. For the quality of owning freezes you forever into 'I' and cuts you off forever from the 'we.'"

As the novel progressed, all other distractions fell away. Pat Covici went to work as a senior editor at the Viking Press, carrying Steinbeck's contracts with him. Viking would publish the collection of Steinbeck stories called *The Long Valley* and would repay any royalties lost during Covici's bankruptcy. For the first time Steinbeck had a publisher whose financial resources were not stretched dangerously thin. Steinbeck and Carol purchased the fifty-acre farm and began construction of a new house. While the house was being built, they lived in one of the property's older structures, a ranch shack that they planned eventually to renovate. Steinbeck also commissioned the installation of a swimming pool for Carol. The pool was intended as a present to show Steinbeck's appreciation for Carol's years of support and belief. They both hoped that in the new house they would be able to repair their marriage.

In September 1938, *The Long Valley* was published by Viking. The short story collection contained the stories of the Tiflin family, as well as almost all of Steinbeck's other short pieces. *The Long Valley* sold well, establishing itself for a time on the nation's best-seller lists. Steinbeck, preoccupied with his long novel, barely noticed his collection's success. He was pushing hard on the story of the Joads and anticipated completing the book before the end of the year. Not even the chaos surrounding the construction of the new house could slow the pace of the book's composition. Carol began typing clean pages from Steinbeck's ledger. She quickly caught up with Steinbeck and was typing pages as soon as he finished writing them. Carol was as delighted with the new novel as was Steinbeck himself. The same month *The Long Valley* was published, Carol came up with the perfect title for her husband's new novel. The book would be called *The Grapes of Wrath*.

As he neared the conclusion of the novel, Steinbeck brought all of the book's elements—migration, nature, homelessness, injustice, courage, anger, and hope—together for a climax that would, he knew, prove controversial. Tom Joad, preparing in the name of self-preservation to take flight from his family, delivers a speech to his mother that would become one of the most famous speeches in American literature. In his speech Tom Joad gives voice to Steinbeck's thoughts not only about the economic and emotional crisis that gripped the world, but also to the larger question of the nature of the collective human soul:

"Tom laughed uneasily. 'Well, maybe . . . a fella ain't got a soul of his own, but only a piece of a big one—an' then'"

" 'Then what, Tom?' "

" 'Then it don' matter. Then I'll be aroun' in the dark. I'll be ever'where—wherever you look. Wherever they's a fight so hungry people can eat. I'll be there. Wherever they's a cop beatin' up a guy, I'll be there . . . why, I'll be in the way guys yell when they're mad an'—I'll be in the way kids laugh when they're hungry an' they know supper's ready. An' when our folks eat the stuff they raise an' live in the houses they build—why, I'll be there. See?' "

Tom leaves his family, fleeing unfair prosecution. Steinbeck did not end the book with Tom's departure, however. He brought the book to a close on a note whose controversy would far exceed that prompted by Tom's speech or by any of the other elements in the novel. With Tom gone, the remaining members of the family are beset by violent weather and personal tragedy. Rose of Sharon, abandoned by her husband, loses her child. In a heavy rainstorm the Joads encounter a starving man. The stranger's plight is more hopeless even than that of the Joads.

Rose of Sharon, on the book's final pages, takes the stranger to her breast to nourish him with the milk for which she has no child other than her fellow human beings. It was a risky, passionate, powerful, symbolic note on which to end so large and ambitious a novel. Steinbeck was enormously proud of the scene, and of *The Grapes of Wrath.*

His pride would not allow him to hold out large commercial hopes for the novel, however. Steinbeck worried that Covici's plans for a large first printing would result in embarrassment and financial loss. In November 1938, not long after Steinbeck finished the book, Covici visited California. The editor did what he could to convince Steinbeck that *The Grapes of Wrath* would be the biggest success yet. All else had been prelude to this, Steinbeck's greatest novel. A month later Elizabeth Otis arrived in California to work with Steinbeck on some of Viking's requests for moderation of the novel's strong language and brutality. Steinbeck was unyielding. He could not take words, however obscene they might be considered by some, out of the mouths of characters for whom such language was not foul but completely natural and appropriate.

He was equally inflexible about the book's final scene, which Covici felt was too symbolic, too abrupt. The novel did not end on a strong note after a careful resolution. It just stopped. Steinbeck tried to explain that he had no interest in literary niceties. His purpose in writing *The Grapes of Wrath* had been to stir readers from their complacency. The breast-feeding scene that ended the novel was, he wrote Covici in some annoyance, true to reality and history, no matter how improper it seemed as a literary device. Rose of Sharon became in the final scene the mother of all the earth, renewing the world with her compassion and love. If readers wanted any more resolution than that, they would have to provide it themselves. Steinbeck was not going to wrap up all of the novel's loose ends just to keep readers and critics happy. Life itself, he reminded his editor, does not often provide neat and satisfactory endings. Neither would John Steinbeck. Covici scheduled the book for publication in March 1939.

Early in the year Steinbeck was elected to the National Institute of Arts and Letters, whose small and carefully chosen membership was composed of the finest and most influential American writers. The election reminded Steinbeck of his high public profile as well as his high level of achievement. He was famous now, and that fame would grow wildly as a result of *The Grapes of Wrath*. Steinbeck reconciled himself as best he could to the attention. Pat Covici was using all of Viking's resources to promote the novel and its author. While Steinbeck insisted on having a hand in the physical design of the book—he had Covici publish the complete lyrics of the "Battle Hymn of the Republic" on the endpapers inside the book's front and back covers—he would not help with the publicity. Occasional interviews were painful enough for Steinbeck. Any sort of promotional tour involving autographs and appearances would overwhelm him. *The Grapes of Wrath* must stand or fall on its own strengths.

That the long novel which Steinbeck had written so swiftly could stand very well on its own became clear throughout the spring of 1939. *The Grapes of Wrath* was published in March and shot instantly to the top of all best-seller lists. Viking was shipping copies by the tens of thousands, unable to keep up with booksellers' orders. Within the first two months more than eighty thousand copies were sold. Film rights to the story were purchased by Twentieth Century Fox for close to a hundred thousand dollars. Book review pages were filled with Steinbeck's name. The early reviews applauded *The Grapes of Wrath* as a work of social and political realism, but also expressed the anticipated reservations about Steinbeck's sense of structure. Few reviewers cared for the symbolic ending. The literary reviews, which appeared later than those in newspapers and large-circulation magazines, surprised Steinbeck by endorsing his novel as a work of art. *North American Review*, which had first published Steinbeck's stories, compared *The Grapes of Wrath* to *Moby-Dick* and *Don Quixote*, and their alumnus to Melville and Cervantes.

The novel was popular, but it was also controversial. Book review sections might endorse the book's success, but many editorial pages attacked the novel and its author. Some editorialists damned Steinbeck's realism as radical and inflammatory. Negative reaction was particularly severe in California's agricultural areas and in many of Oklahoma's cities. People in both states felt that Steinbeck had maligned them. Some California farmers' groups worked to have the novel banned from schools and public libraries. Steinbeck's language, and his novel's blunt approach and presentation of sexuality, also sparked outrage. *The Grapes of Wrath* was condemned in many churches and civic meetings as impure and immoral. Across the country, movements started to have the book prohibited. Many librarians, unwilling to take a firm stand and forbid the book from their shelves, simply refused to purchase copies. An outraged California society woman, Ruth Comfort Mitchell, wrote a novel herself to rebut Steinbeck's horrid novel. Mitchell's book was called *Of Human Kindness* and did not sell well. Behind the public attacks on Steinbeck flowed a current of malicious innuendo and gossip, aimed at ruining Steinbeck's name. Steinbeck's book, though, had impressed far more people than it offended. In early summer the First Lady, Eleanor Roosevelt, used her newspaper column to issue a public statement calling *The Grapes of Wrath* "an unforgettable experience in reading." Mrs. Roosevelt even went so far as to praise the novel's final scene as beautiful.

By summer Steinbeck knew that the excitement created by his novel was not going to fade quickly. Sales were increasing toward ten thousand copies a week. His mail was simply stacked and ignored; there was no way Steinbeck could answer every letter and appeal even if he wanted to. The ranch offered less privacy than he and Carol had hoped. The excitement of working together as *The Grapes of Wrath* was being written had worn off. The new house and pool, the vast sums of money coming in, the freedom to travel widely and indulge whims—none of the benefits of Steinbeck's success could ease the tension between himself and his wife. He and Carol fought constantly and bitterly. Carol was drinking heavily. Sometimes Steinbeck also looked for distraction in alcohol, often in the company of Ed Ricketts. He spent long hours in Ricketts's laboratory, studying scientific texts and listening to selections from the biologist's large collection of classical music albums. Steinbeck and Ricketts spoke of getting away from Monterey, of losing themselves in the hard work of a scientific expedition.

When Steinbeck did get away it was to Hollywood. Two films based on his books were in production there. *The Grapes of Wrath* was being filmed under the direction of John Ford. The motion picture would star Henry Fonda, who had been Steinbeck's own preference for the role of Tom Joad, although the studio had first wanted Tyrone Power to play the part. *Of Mice and Men* was also in front of the cameras, with Lewis Milestone directing. Burgess Meredith played George, and Lon Chaney, Jr.—not yet typecast as a horror film star—played the giant, mentally deficient Lennie. Steinbeck took an apartment in Hollywood, ostensibly to help with the screen adaptations of his books, but also to escape from the tensions of his failing marriage.

Steinbeck hoped to use his Hollywood isolation as a period of recuperation and revitalization. His circle of Hollywood friends expanded. In addition to Charles Chaplin, Steinbeck became close with Henry Fonda, Burgess Meredith, and Spencer Tracy. Steinbeck did not often socialize outside his apartment. Since completing *The Grapes of Wrath* he had been in nearly constant pain as a result of inflamed nerves in his legs. Some days he could barely walk. Steinbeck purchased a diathermy machine, which he used to apply heat to the most painful areas. Steinbeck's friends worried about him, and about

the wisdom of his trying to treat the neuritis himself. Acquaintances and friends took to dropping by the apartment to offer
what cheer they could. Sometimes they brought guests whom
they thought the author would enjoy meeting. One such guest
was Gwendolyn Conger, an attractive, twenty-year-old woman.
Steinbeck found himself drawn to Gwyn, as she preferred her
name to be spelled. She was embarked upon a not very successful career as a singer and actress and was full of enthusiasm
for life. Steinbeck and Gwyn saw each other frequently during
the summer of 1939, but Steinbeck restrained himself from a
serious romance. Too many questions were unsettled in his
marriage.

Things were getting no better at the ranch near Los Gatos.
Carol's moods had become more and more unpredictable. One
day she might work hard and with focused concentration on
investing the money they were earning, the next day she would
return to her drinking and gleefully paint a piano bright pink.
Steinbeck had dedicated *The Grapes of Wrath* in part to Carol
and in part to Thomas Collins, who had helped him with research in the migrant camps. His debt to Collins was paid now,
but he could not escape the larger responsibility he owed the
woman who had for so long believed in him. As fall neared, he
tried to spend more time with her. He felt that if he could
impose some order on his life, and upon the success that was
disrupting it, he might be able at least to make an environment
in which Carol could come to grips with her emotional problems. Steinbeck was not yet ready to end the marriage.

He was less certain about his career as a novelist. For nearly
a year he had been the most successful member of that profession in the world. As Christmas approached the sales figures for
The Grapes of Wrath continued to rise. Newspapers, magazines,
and public gatherings were no less filled with Steinbeck's name
than when the book was first published. An ongoing national
debate raged around *The Grapes of Wrath*. The book was formally banned in East St. Louis, Illinois, and copies publicly

burned there. Immorality and vulgarity remained the charges most frequently aimed at the novel. Even the praise for the book and the quickly completed motion picture missed the point, Steinbeck felt. Everyone focused upon the social realism and criticism. The motion picture ended with Henry Fonda's stirring rendition of Tom Joad's final speech, followed by a moment of sentimental Hollywood hopefulness. Despite the false note at the end, the motion picture was true to Steinbeck's spirit and brought huge numbers of new readers into contact with his work. Most of those readers responded to the plight of the migrants, of the Okies cast from their homes.

Steinbeck had written, however, not about that plight alone. Few readers or reviewers gave any indication of having perceived the philosophy that lay beneath the surface of Steinbeck's novel. *The Grapes of Wrath* reflected its author's concern for society, but it also represented his largest attempt yet to give literary form to his theories of the phalanx. Steinbeck felt that he had to attack the subject once more, yet was not certain how to go about it. In the year since he completed the novel, he had written nothing of lasting value, and very little other than letters. Now it seemed to him that since he could not stop the attention that *The Grapes of Wrath* had provoked, he must simply learn to ignore it. He had work to get on with and was impatient about the time he was wasting. He began gathering his energy and determination. His thoughts seemed to grow more calm. As 1939 ended, the most famous novelist in the world felt that he had completely written himself out of fiction. His only hope of continuing to function as a writer was to find a whole new way of writing.

SEVEN
EXPEDITIONS

BEFORE STEINBECK COULD BEGIN to write the sorts of new books he planned, he had to lay their foundation. He intended to approach philosophy by way of science and, by the first of January 1940, was spending most of his time studying texts and taking notes. Steinbeck had cause to regret his youthful indolence at Stanford—there were great gaps in his education. For years he had considered himself a serious amateur naturalist and collector, yet now Steinbeck realized how little he actually knew of the basic history and process of science. With Ed Ricketts guiding his reading, Steinbeck immersed himself in re-education. He and Carol divided their time between Los Gatos and Pacific Grove, with Steinbeck staying at Ricketts's laboratories for long hours. During the time they spent together, Steinbeck and Ricketts began working toward the goal of a scientific expedition, one result of which would be a collaborative book. Thanks to the success of *The Grapes of Wrath*, Steinbeck could afford to underwrite an expedition of some ambition. In preparation, he, Carol, and Ricketts went on several collecting trips along the California coast. As they traveled, worked, read, and talked together, the larger expedition took shape. The group would charter a vessel in the spring and equip it for a lengthy examination of marine invertebrates in the littoral of the Gulf of California.

The new work invigorated Steinbeck. His neuritis bothered him less, and he felt stronger than he had in years. He was learning a great deal very quickly, applying himself to his studies with far more discipline than he had managed in college. Ed Ricketts was a good teacher. Together, Ricketts and Steinbeck pursued scientific points on into philosophy, their debates lasting long into the night. Marine invertebrate biology was only a starting place for their discussions. Because they both saw the universe in ecological terms, with all of its aspects part of the same, single system, Steinbeck and Ricketts allowed themselves to seek great truths from small observations. They planned several collaborations. Certainly there would be an account of the long collecting trip. With luck they would make some discoveries and thus produce a book that would make a genuine contribution to serious science. Nor would popular audiences be neglected by the literary partnership between Steinbeck and Ricketts. Steinbeck began making notes and plans for handbooks to be written for lay readers, those who lacked advanced scientific training. It occurred to both that out of all of the work would come some philosophical writing as well. Neither Pat Covici nor Elizabeth Otis were excited about the new direction Steinbeck was taking. Steinbeck did not hear their hesitation. He felt drawn to his ledgers more strongly than ever. It was as if everything he had written so far was in preparation for the exhausting, exhilarating work he had now undertaken.

Some of the preparation was just fun. Steinbeck and Ricketts devoted a good deal of time and thought to the selection of the right boat. They spent hours on the docks in Monterey, examining fishing vessels spacious enough to accommodate lab tables, specimen jars, and preserving chemicals, as well as provisions. Steinbeck's fascination with well-made and well-run machinery benefited them. He distrusted any boat whose engine room was not spotless, confessing to a belief in an almost mystical bond between engine and operator. When they discovered boats that were suitable for their purposes, Steinbeck and

Ricketts often encountered resistance from the boat owners. A biological expedition made little sense to many of the hard, practical sardine fishermen. It took weeks for Steinbeck and Ricketts to come into contact with a willing shipmaster, but finally they met Anthony Berry. Berry was intrigued by the plan. Steinbeck and Ricketts chartered Berry's *Western Flyer* and began assembling a crew. The *Western Flyer* was seventy-six feet long and was equipped with a lovely, immaculately maintained engine. They would set out in March.

Occasionally Steinbeck stole time from the preparations and returned to Hollywood. He was a man of some prestige there now. Both *The Grapes of Wrath* and *Of Mice and Men* were box office successes. Steinbeck himself was enormously pleased with both pictures. The trips to Hollywood also permitted Steinbeck to visit Gwyn Conger. Steinbeck's delight in her company continued to grow. Although he tried to remain tentative in his relationship with Gwyn, he knew that he was falling in love. As the start of the expedition neared, Steinbeck stayed close to Monterey. All of the excitement of packing the *Western Flyer* distracted him from the guilt he felt over Gwyn. He and Carol made extra efforts to work together well. Quarters aboard the *Western Flyer* would be close; domestic difficulties would interfere with the hard scientific work that lay ahead. On March 11, Steinbeck, Carol, and Ricketts joined Berry and his crew on board the *Western Flyer*. A raucous bon voyage party delayed the planned morning departure until early afternoon. Once under way the *Western Flyer* showed her ability to make good speed and handle seas well. Steinbeck set up his bunk in the engine room and slept deeply, lulled by the sounds of the engine.

After taking on final provisions in San Diego, the charter passed south of the Mexican border. For nearly a week the boat ran south along the coast of Lower California. Steinbeck was fascinated by the way the water deepened in color, becoming a rich blue that teemed with life. He stood for hours on deck, absorbing every detail of the seascape. To save time, the *Western Flyer* sped onward day and night. Steinbeck thought of Charles Darwin and envied the great naturalist the more leisurely pace mandated by the age of sail. Steinbeck could happily have spent days at any point along the route, collecting specimens, recording observations, defining an ecology. Although they collected some specimens as they fared south, the primary destination was the Gulf of California. The more time they saved getting there, the more comprehensive their examination of the littoral's ecology would be. By the seventeenth, the *Western Flyer* had rounded the peninsula's southernmost point. Steinbeck saw that even a well-bounded body of water such as this would be impossible to catalog in a trip of only a few weeks. He referred to the Gulf by its original, Spanish name, the Sea of Cortez.

The vast variety of littoral invertebrates was daunting. Ricketts kept the expedition constantly on the move. They all worked double and triple shifts, just to keep up with the labeling of their samples. In addition to scientific records, Steinbeck kept notes toward the book he and Ricketts would write. As well as a scientific account of the findings, Steinbeck wanted to put together a volume that would provide the reader with a sense of the natural environment in which the specimens lived. He wanted readers to know how the air tasted when he collected an anemone. He wanted them to feel the salt spray as the *Western Flyer* pushed on to another collecting site. Such a book would combine science, poetry, and philosophy, producing a mixture unlike anything Steinbeck had ever read:

"We collected down the littoral as the water went down. We didn't seem to have time enough. We took samples of everything that came to hand. The uppermost rocks swarmed with Sally Lightfoots, those beautiful and fast and sensitive crabs. With them were white periwinkle snails. Below that, barnacles and Purpura snails; more crabs and many limpets. Below that many serpulids—attached worms in calcereous tubes with beautiful purple foliate heads. Below that, the multi-rayed starfish, *He-*

liaster kubiniji of Xanthus. . . . In the lowest surf-levels there was a brilliant gathering of the moss animals known as bryozoa; flatworms; flat crabs; the large sea cucumber; some anemones; many sponges of two types, a smooth, encrusting purple one, the other erect, white, and calcereous. There were great colonies of tunicates, clusters of tiny individuals joined by a common tunic and looking so like the sponges that even a trained worker must await the specialist's determination to know whether his find is sponge or tunicate. This is annoying, for the sponge being one step above the protozoa, at the bottom of the evolutionary ladder, and the tunicate near the top, your trained worker is likely to feel that a dirty trick has been played upon him by an entirely too democratic Providence."

Providence, or the universe's lack thereof, was much on the group's mind. When they were not working, they talked. Steinbeck, his wife, and his closest friend launched themselves into freewheeling discussions after work was done. Speculative thinking, the more speculative the better, was prized among the conversationalists on board the *Western Flyer*. These thought experiments allowed them to extend what they were learning about the littoral of the Sea of Cortez to all of life, to all of creation. The nature of that creation came to occupy the center of their thoughts. The Steinbecks and Ricketts devoted many of their discussions to *teleology*, a philosophical system that, basically, seeks to ascribe a purpose to the evolution of the universe and its life. The *purpose*, for example, of lower life forms is to provide food for higher species. The purpose of the universe is to provide a home for living things; the purpose of living things is to inhabit the universe. Teleology underlay most religions, much of the arts and sciences. Its outlook was anathema to Steinbeck. He began developing nonteleological arguments, which he would distill into the book about the Sea of Cortez expedition.

Steinbeck felt that there was no guided or directed purpose to the universe. Such ideas, in fact, struck him as dangerous.

They were dishonest, based more on hopefulness than on hard, realistic observation. Teleology made for dangerous political thinking as well. A teleologist, he reflected, saw leaders as those who give instruction and direction to their followers. Steinbeck himself had sought to refute that notion in *The Grapes of Wrath*. Leaders, he felt, were the results of mass movements. The readers and reviewers had missed his point in the novel. Perhaps science would give him the opportunity to make his case more clearly. Nonteleological thinking would guide the composition of the record of the collecting trip. The book would contain examples and discussions of the conclusions Steinbeck and Ricketts reached. The examples would make dramatic the patterns of nature. From those patterns, Steinbeck believed, nonteleological conclusions were the only sorts of truths that could be found:

"All night the hissing rush and splash of hunters and hunted went on. We had never been in water so heavily populated. The light, piercing the surface, showed the water almost solid with fish—swarming, hungry, frantic fish, incredible in their voraciousness. The schools swam, marshaled and patrolled. They turned as a unit and dived as a unit. In their millions they followed a pattern minute as to depth and direction and speed. There must be some fallacy in our thinking of these fish as individuals. Their functions in the school are in some as yet unknown way as controlled as though the school were one unit. We cannot conceive of this intricacy until we are able to think of the school as an animal itself, reacting with all its cells to stimuli which might not influence one fish at all. . . . In the little Bay of San Carlos, where there were many schools of a number of species, there was even a feeling (and 'feeling' is used advisedly) of a larger unit which was the interrelation of species with their interdependence for food, even though that food be each other. A smoothly working larger animal surviving within itself—larval shrimp to little fish to larger fish to giant fish—one operating mechanism. And perhaps *this* unit of survival may key into the larger animal which is the life of all the sea, and this into the larger of the world. There would seem to be only one commandment for living things: Survive! And the forms and species and units and groups are armed for survival, fanged for survival, timid for it, fierce for it, clever for it, poisonous for it, intelligent for it. This commandment decrees the death and destruction of myriads of individuals for the survival of the whole. Life has one final end, to be alive; and all the tricks and mechanisms, all the successes and all the failures, are aimed at that end."

The group instinct so carefully observed in marine life was also evident on shore. Steinbeck found a strong German presence in the Mexican ports at which the *Western Flyer* paid call. In Europe, as the Sea of Cortez undertaking proceeded, the Nazis were on the march, overrunning France and much of Scandinavia. In Mexico the Nazi message was delivered not by tanks, troops, and bombers, but by propaganda. If the Nazis could rally the support of the Mexican people, the United States would be forced to use its resources for the defense of its own borders rather than for the aid of those nations under direct Nazi attack in Europe. Steinbeck was concerned. He saw no evidence of American countermeasures. Steinbeck added political notes and ideas to his files and began to consider the best way to deliver his message to officials in Washington.

By April 20, 1940, the journey was ended. The *Western Flyer* was once more docked in Monterey. Ricketts and Steinbeck supervised the off-loading of their specimens. Ricketts was eager to begin arranging their findings and photographs for publication, but Steinbeck could not concentrate on the book. Little more than a month passed before he was back in Mexico, this time at work on a film script for a movie that he would, in part, produce. The film was to be a documentary about life in a traditional Mexican village. Steinbeck insisted that the motion picture deal with the conflict between superstition and science, and gave the documentary a narrative. He called his script *The*

Forgotten Village and in the simplest language told the story of a people torn between tradition and the need for modern medicines. The script was barely three dozen handwritten pages long. He and Carol stayed in Mexico City as the script was developed. Steinbeck was once more struck by the force and pervasiveness of the Nazi propaganda. Back in the United States in June, he traveled to Washington and sent his concerns by letter to President Roosevelt.

Steinbeck's name carried greater weight than ever. *The Grapes of Wrath* had just been announced as the recipient of the Pulitzer Prize. Roosevelt invited Steinbeck to the White House to discuss the author's Mexican observations. Steinbeck, aware of the power of motion pictures, recommended that the government endorse the use of motion pictures for outright propaganda and thus beat the Nazis at their own game. Roosevelt listened politely to Steinbeck's suggestions, but did not turn them into policy.

The collaboration with Ed Ricketts continued to give Steinbeck difficulty. Ricketts felt that Steinbeck was not paying proper attention to the book about their scientific adventure. Covici urged Steinbeck to write another novel, rather than a book that would sell only a fraction as many copies as a work of fiction. Steinbeck's relationship with Carol continued to collapse. He arranged many meetings with Gwyn Conger, and they developed a series of codes by which they could leave secret messages for each other. Often they met at Carol's cottage in a canyon near Los Angeles. Steinbeck was tormented by the deception and worried as well by Carol's ill health and depression. The production of *The Forgotten Village* made demands on Steinbeck's time that Ricketts bitterly resented. Steinbeck divided his time between Monterey and Mexico. In the fall he returned briefly to Washington for another meeting with President Roosevelt. This time Steinbeck suggested to him that the United States begin producing large quantities of counterfeit

German currency that could be scattered behind Nazi lines in hopes of ruining the German economy. The plan attracted some excitement in Washington, but was never put into effect.

It was January 1941, before Steinbeck got down to consistent work on his portion of the Sea of Cortez book. He and Carol separated for two months, with Carol vacationing in Hawaii. Gwyn Conger came to Monterey for long visits, and Steinbeck traveled to Los Angeles occasionally. For all that, he was soon producing manuscript at the rate of several thousand words a day. Collaboration did not come easily to Steinbeck. Despite his studious efforts, he was not scientist enough to participate fully in the annotated catalog portions of the book, although his style and personality can be found in some of the notes. Nor was Ricketts completely comfortable in writing narrative. The two debated and argued over the form of the book, each absorbing the other's point of view while compensating for the other's weaknesses. Steinbeck strived for the most precise language he'd ever used. He and Ricketts thrashed out their philosophical differences. The power of nonteleological thinking formed the center of their narrative. This outlook lay behind everything in the book, and its authors' convictions took center stage in long, reflective, philosophical passages.

Away from his desk, Steinbeck found reflection impossible. When Carol returned from Hawaii in April, Steinbeck revealed to her his affair with Gwyn. In fact, Gwyn joined the Steinbecks almost immediately. The confrontation was angry and tearful. Both women claimed to be carrying Steinbeck's child. For a time Steinbeck swore off Gwyn, but before April was out, it was clear that he and Carol were finished. Steinbeck retired to the cottage at Pacific Grove. In that community, where he and Carol had spent so many of their early days together, he managed to complete his work on the narrative portion of the marine biology book. There remained a good deal of work to be done on the manuscript, but Steinbeck was unable to devote more than partial attention to it. A number of responsibilities and projects tugged at him.

Primary among them was Carol. Under the terms of their separation, she received one thousand dollars each month. She had not yet formally filed for divorce, but Steinbeck knew that when she did it would be expensive. The Los Gatos ranch was sold by late summer. An accounting was made of Steinbeck's finances and holdings. He was eager for a fair settlement of his assets, planning to give Carol at least half of his earnings on books written during their marriage. Steinbeck's old friend Webster Street agreed to handle the legal proceedings as Carol reconciled herself to divorce.

The Forgotten Village also occupied Steinbeck's time. Filming had been completed the previous fall. A picture book reproducing Steinbeck's spare script along with black-and-white stills from the movie had been published by Viking in May 1941. In October, with the film set to open in East Coast theaters, the New York State Board of Censors found *The Forgotten Village* to be obscene and prohibited its showing. The film, in its honest depiction of peasant life, included images of childbirth and nursing, which New York's censors would not allow the public to see. Steinbeck traveled East and threw himself into the battle. Eleanor Roosevelt also attempted to intercede on behalf of the honest little film. It was winter before the ban was lifted, and the movie was all but forgotten in the excitement and uncertainty following the Japanese attack on Pearl Harbor.

The collaboration between Steinbeck and Ricketts, which was far more dangerous to contemporary minds and morals, faced no censorship. Its commercial prospects, slim in the best of times, were further reduced by the war. Published shortly before the Japanese attack, it bore the title *Sea of Cortez: A Leisurely Journal of Travel and Exploration.* A series of beautiful color plates in the center of the long book was followed by dozens of black-and-white drawings, photographs, and charts.

The narrative account of the adventure filled nearly half the book, with the rest composed of closely written phyletic notes and references which cataloged the group's findings and specimens. The title page showed the authors as equal collaborators: John Steinbeck and Edward F. Ricketts.

Collaboration of another sort was on Steinbeck's mind as the first year of the war began. In the fall he had begun work on a new piece of fiction, a play in which he portrayed an American town conquered by a totalitarian enemy. Part of the focus of the play was directed at the portrayal of collaborators, traitors. Steinbeck balanced that with an underground resistance movement against which no army, however mechanized and efficient, could survive forever. Steinbeck called his play *The Moon Is Down*. He wrote the play quickly and early in the new year completed a second draft which moved the action to an unnamed but obviously Scandinavian country. Steinbeck wanted only to give an accurate representation of human behavior. His objectivity demanded that he show both conqueror and conquered as human beings; his philosophy turned the characters into members of groups that were themselves part of larger groups. Steinbeck also wrote a version of *The Moon Is Down* as a short novel, which Viking scheduled for spring publication.

When the book appeared in March, it was clear that the public attraction to Steinbeck's work had not died down. His new novel was nearly as big a success as *The Grapes of Wrath*. Viking sold nearly a hundred thousand copies of *The Moon Is Down* before the book's official publication day, despite ha.sh and sometimes hostile reviews. Steinbeck's objectivity, derived more from his scientific studies than from traditional literature, was misunderstood once again. The cartoonist James Thurber denounced Steinbeck for writing a book that was sympathetic to the Nazis. Other critics sounded similar notes. The public, though, knew better. Readers recognized and responded to the human drama and truth in *The Moon Is Down*, lifting the printings of trade and book club editions close to three hundred thousand copies in barely a month.

The play opened in April to reviews similar to the novel's. Audiences, however, were large, and before the month was out, motion picture rights were purchased for well over a hundred thousand dollars. Even more gratifying was the news from Europe that the Nazis, whom Steinbeck's critics said he sympathized with, feared the book. In occupied countries a person could be executed for having a copy of John Steinbeck's *The Moon Is Down*. Such threats did not stop the book from being circulated in crudely printed and even handwritten editions.

Steinbeck wanted to join the war effort in more than literary fashion. The nation was mobilizing its resources as never before, showing Steinbeck his phalanx most dramatically. He wanted to march with that phalanx into combat, but his government had other plans for him. By the spring of 1942, after a meeting with Franklin Roosevelt, Steinbeck was involved in writing a book about American bombers and their crews. On assignment from the Air Corps, Steinbeck spent a month rising at dawn with Air Corps trainees and sharing the routine of their military education. He had taken flying lessons earlier in his life, but now found himself aloft for most of each day. Steinbeck, surrounded by efficient men who formed well-organized groups, enjoyed himself immensely. By the end of summer he had completed a small book about the Air Corps. It was called *Bombs Away: The Story of a Bomber Team*. Steinbeck donated his earnings from the book to a military charity.

Soon he was at work on a more commercial piece of propaganda. Twentieth Century Fox, like all of Hollywood's studios, was producing a number of films that served as entertainment and as patriotic calls for unity against the Axis. Steinbeck was signed to write a script based on the desperate, dangerous battle against German submarines, which were sinking many Allied ships. Specifically, Steinbeck's script would deal with the survivors of a torpedo attack, a group of individuals brought together in a lifeboat. Alfred Hitchcock would direct the film. Steinbeck had previously encountered Hollywood only as an outsider whose work was being adapted. *The Forgotten Village* had been an independent production in which Steinbeck had invested his own money. Now he served as a screenwriter working with a major studio and a renowned director. He learned quickly that although the words spoken on screen were created by the writer, it was the director and the producer who held the real power in Hollywood. Steinbeck was pleased with his original script for *Lifeboat*. He had managed to sound the call for arms while also telling an exciting story and presenting insights about the functioning of groups. Hitchcock made many changes that angered Steinbeck. *Lifeboat*, when it appeared the following year, was a polished, frivolous film filled with what Steinbeck considered to be racist innuendo. Disillusioned long before the filming was completed, Steinbeck was ready to get out of Hollywood. He and Gwyn moved to New York.

In March 1943, Steinbeck's divorce became final, and he was free to marry Gwyn Conger. They had been living together since Steinbeck and Carol had separated, and they were married within a few weeks of the divorce decree. Steinbeck and Gwyn settled in a comfortable house outside New York City. Their marriage was only a couple of months old when Steinbeck was cleared to travel to combat zones as a war correspondent. He announced that he was ready to go overseas immediately. Steinbeck would file his stories on assignment with the New York *Herald Tribune*; abroad, the pieces would appear in London's *Daily Express*. Gwyn was displeased. She tried to dissuade Steinbeck from his plans by telling him that she was pregnant. Her claim was no more true now than earlier. Steinbeck ignored Gwyn's anger as much as he could and in early June set sail for England. He filed his first piece quickly, and with it made clear that he would bring not only his talent but also his special concerns to his journalism:

"The troops in their thousands sit on their equipment on the dock. It is evening, and the first of the dimout lights come on. The men wear their helmets, which make them all look alike, make them look like long rows of mushrooms. Their rifles are leaning against their knees. They have no identity, no personality. The men are units in an army. The numbers chalked on their helmets are almost like the license numbers on robots."

For nearly four months Steinbeck absorbed material and transformed it into clearly written newspaper pieces. He had no trouble finding stories, and the stories he wrote attracted attention and comment. He was able to give readers at home a real sense of the human cost of the war, reminding his audience that faceless armies were composed of individuals. Some of the other journalists, whose names and works were less celebrated than Steinbeck's, were jealous of his abilities. Steinbeck created word portraits that held no real news, yet somehow told more truth about the war than pages of straightforward reporting. After filing eight weeks' worth of human interest dispatches from England, Steinbeck was ready to see some real action. He wanted to join the phalanx in battle.

He got his chance in September. After a trip to North Africa, Steinbeck spent several harrowing, exhilarating nights onboard PT boats off the coast of Italy. The boats were harassing German installations north of Naples in an attempt to convince the Nazis that an invasion was forthcoming. Later in the month Steinbeck moved south, joining the Allied forces at the actual invasion site, the beaches at Salerno. The invading army met heavy resistance from German artillery and machine guns. Steinbeck now saw war close up, watching as newly arrived young men became hardened veterans in a matter of hours. The brutality and senselessness of combat moved Steinbeck profoundly. He was in awe of the courage displayed by the American troops. Steinbeck displayed courage of his own, as well as a willingness to break the rules and conventions by which correspondents were bound. Steinbeck often removed his war correspondent's badge to take up a weapon. He encountered a friend from Hollywood, Douglas Fairbanks, Jr., who was now leading small detachments of commandos on night raids against Nazi radar facilities. On the raids Steinbeck performed as a commando himself and acquitted himself well in dangerous situations.

The *Herald Tribune* was pleased with Steinbeck's work and encouraged him to continue reporting from Europe. But Steinbeck was ready to return to the United States. He had accomplished all the goals he'd set himself, learning about combat and proving himself equal to its challenges. He had seen men and women rise to the heights of heroism and had seen others fall, their bodies shattered by shrapnel. Steinbeck knew that those he observed and wrote about were participants in a mass movement whose end result would be the liberation of Europe from Nazi tyranny. He also knew that the price paid not only in the lives of soldiers but also in the lives of civilians including innocent children was enormous. Somehow he would have to accommodate his new experiences and insights in his writing. He was ready to return to fiction.

EIGHT

LOW EBB

STEINBECK WAS BACK IN New York before Thanksgiving 1943. His relations with Gwyn were strained at first. In some ways she had not forgiven him for abandoning her so soon after their marriage. Her letters while Steinbeck was overseas were filled with references to various maladies and illnesses. The fact that Steinbeck seemed distant did not help Gwyn's attitude. Steinbeck was reeling from his experiences in Europe. His sleep was troubled, his thoughts haunted with images of the destruction and death he had seen. There was no easy way for Steinbeck to overcome his preoccupation with war and death. He completed the pieces still owed the *Herald Tribune* and, with his desk clear, began making notes for a new novel. Rather than write about the horrors he'd witnessed, Steinbeck began a novel about a marine biologist living on the waterfront in Monterey. It was a funny novel, not terribly ambitious, filled with humorous anecdotes and insights and a love of life that some would find reminiscent of *Tortilla Flat*. Steinbeck called the new book *Cannery Row*.

He was also planning an even simpler, yet more somber story about a Mexican peasant's discovery of a priceless pearl. Thoughts of Mexico made Steinbeck nostalgic for that country and its people. In April 1944, he and Gwynn took a long vacation in Mexico City. They celebrated the fact that Gwyn was, at last, actually pregnant. The baby was due in late summer. Steinbeck, at forty-two, was somewhat concerned about his ability to make the adjustments required of a parent. Some days he felt older than his years. His hair was shot with gray, and occasionally his neuritis flared up. Steinbeck's hearing had been damaged by the concussion from artillery shells at Salerno. His eyes were weakening perceptibly. Gwyn, on the other hand, had never looked more beautiful. Their trip to Mexico proved restful. In the spring Steinbeck returned to New York rejuvenated and ready to work.

He picked up on *Cannery Row* and soon was producing more than a thousand words a day. He knew that the book was nowhere near so ambitious as had been *The Grapes of Wrath*, yet the slightness of his new work did not bother him. The celebrity that resulted from his great novel had enabled Steinbeck to gain audience with President Roosevelt, to acquire plum correspondent assignments and opportunities, and to live well while paying Carol a handsome alimony. All of the advantages were outweighed by Steinbeck's distaste for personal fame. *The Moon Is Down* had proved a surprising success. Now, though, five years had passed since the publication of *The Grapes of Wrath*, and Steinbeck began to hope that some of the public attention would fade. A short, funny book might help readers establish some sense of perspective about John Steinbeck and his accomplishments.

Steinbeck and Gwyn settled in an apartment on East Fifty-first Street. By midsummer Steinbeck was nearly finished with *Cannery Row*. Discussions were proceeding with Steinbeck about turning his story of the peasant and the pearl into a script for a motion picture to be produced in Mexico. Steinbeck was also in touch with Ed Ricketts, who had served in the army during the war but who was now back in Monterey. They were already planning new expeditions and books, and Steinbeck told Gwyn that after the birth of the baby they would move to the West Coast. He was taking notes for a long novel that he intended to write. The big book would be based at least in part on elements of his family history and would be called "The Salinas Valley."

All of Steinbeck's projects were happily interrupted on August 2, 1944, when Gwyn gave birth to a son. The boy was named Thom Steinbeck, although his father referred to him simply as Tom. Steinbeck discovered that fatherhood delighted him. He wrote some funny, touching letters about his pleasure in the new baby, although before Thom was six weeks old Steinbeck was developing theories about the virtues of housing children in cells or pens until they were old enough to be reasoned with. For all of his cynicism, Steinbeck revealed that he wanted more children. He and Gwyn began packing for an October move to Monterey.

Steinbeck completed the manuscript of *Cannery Row* early in the fall. After examining several houses in Monterey, he purchased an adobe home whose grounds allowed him to indulge in a large garden. The house was more than a century old, and its needs in the way of repairs and upkeep appealed to the handyman in Steinbeck. Perhaps best of all was the wall that surrounded the house, giving Steinbeck and his family at least the illusion of privacy. His novel finished, Steinbeck spent days working on the property, finding far more relaxation in wielding a shovel than he had in New York's night life. When he did set up an office for himself, it was at a makeshift table in a woodshed. He continued to work on the story he called "The Pearl," hoping to have a finished film script by the end of the year. Pat Covici wrote from New York that advance sales of *Cannery Row* showed promise of the book's becoming another enormous success. Steinbeck was pleased but anticipated a poor critical reaction.

Both Steinbeck and Covici were proved right. *Cannery Row* was published shortly after the New Year's celebration and became the first smash best-seller of 1945. Viking's first printing of 78,000 copies did not fill even the advance orders. Covici wagered that the short novel would sell a quarter of a million copies, despite a disastrous critical reception. Steinbeck suspected the reviewers of lying in wait for him since the success of *The Grapes of Wrath*. The attacks on *The Moon Is Down* had been focused primarily at Steinbeck's failure as a political thinker. *Cannery Row* was attacked from all sides. Left-wing magazines and newspapers accused Steinbeck of betraying the causes about which he'd once written so passionately. Literary critics simply dismissed the new novel as trivial. *Cannery Row*, some of them sneered, was merely popular storytelling, a commercial book without art or insight. Steinbeck's anticipation of the attacks did not lessen the pain they caused him. But he had written *Cannery Row* on several levels, the least of which was that of popular comedy. The book included beautifully written passages of nature poetry, as well as examinations of such familiar Steinbeck concerns as Arthurian honor and the group consciousness. The critics did not notice or care. Only the public cared, buying *Cannery Row* by the thousands.

Steinbeck hid his disappointment and applied himself once more to the film script of "The Pearl," or "La Perla." He completed the draft late in January and began making plans to return to Mexico for the filming. He also began a prose version of the story, which Viking could publish either as a short novel or as the centerpiece of a collection. Steinbeck was happy about returning to Mexico and suddenly thrilled at the prospect of leaving Monterey. The adobe house and walls, which he hoped would insulate him from the curious, could not keep out the community's hostility. *Cannery Row*, with its cast of drunks, prostitutes, and bums however noble, angered the Monterey establishment even more than *Tortilla Flat* had. Steinbeck and Gwyn were snubbed on the streets, and he even found himself denied trade by many local businesses. By May the Steinbecks were settled in Cuernavaca, Mexico.

Despite the pressures involved in preparing to shoot the film, Steinbeck's creative energies were renewed in Mexico. He quickly completed the narrative version of his story and mailed

The Pearl, as he called it, to his agents. Steinbeck enjoyed more control over the new film than over those he'd been involved with in Hollywood. He immersed himself in technical and cinematic details. Steinbeck at first found it difficult to think in terms of camera placement and lighting, but he learned the mechanics of filmmaking thoroughly and played a large part in establishing the somber look of the film of *The Pearl*. The story was simple. A peasant named Kino discovers a pearl whose size and beauty will make him, his wife, and infant son wealthy. Steinbeck's fable built to a tragic ending, in which Kino discovers that by obtaining great wealth he loses all that is truly valuable in his life. In addition to work on *The Pearl*, Steinbeck began making notes toward a longer novel, his most ambitious since *The Grapes of Wrath*. The new book would deal with a group of people making a journey by bus. Steinbeck intended the story to be openly metaphysical, an allegory in which the story's events would provide a forum for philosophical argument. Steinbeck at first thought of giving the book a Spanish title, "El Camion Vacilador," but came to refer to the book as *The Wayward Bus*. While in Cuernavaca he was also approached to write a motion picture script based upon the life of the Mexican revolutionary Emiliano Zapata.

By late fall the filming of *The Pearl* was nearly complete. Steinbeck was ready to return to the United States, but Monterey had lost its appeal for him. He placed the adobe house on the market. After discussions with Gwyn, who was pregnant again, Steinbeck decided that it was time for them to make a permanent home in New York. The success of *Cannery Row* had replenished Steinbeck's funds. He purchased adjoining brownstone homes on East Seventy-eighth Street. The homes would require a good bit of renovation, much of which Steinbeck planned to accomplish himself. There was garden space behind the homes, and Steinbeck looked forward to working once more with fertile soil, planting vegetables, flowers, and shrubs. Steinbeck, Gwyn, and Thom lived for a while in a small apartment, moving at last into their brownstone in March 1946. The adjoining home would be rented out. Its first tenant was Nathaniel Benchley, a young writer whose father, the famous humorist Robert Benchley, was one of Steinbeck's Hollywood acquaintances.

The new novel gave Steinbeck a great deal of difficulty. His problems with the book were complicated by increasingly strained relations with Gwyn. The long months of pregnancy left her depressed and irritable. She and Steinbeck fought often. Steinbeck established an office for himself in the basement of their brownstone and secluded himself there for long hours of work on *The Wayward Bus*. He wrote thousands of words and threw them all away. Steinbeck knew exactly what he wanted to accomplish with his story, yet he could not make his narrative match his ambitions. He told Pat Covici that although the bus of which he wrote traveled over rutted back roads, its route was really a cosmic one. Steinbeck had an image of his bus rolling across the galaxy, driven by a man who was really a god. There was to be nothing simple or traditional about the symbolism in this new novel. Steinbeck was willing to spend years getting the story exactly right. He originally set the story in Mexico but could not make the work come alive. Gradually he began to think of shifting the setting to more familiar California landscapes.

Steinbeck's second son was born on June 12, 1946. The boy was named John Steinbeck IV. While Gwyn was in the hospital, Steinbeck kept house and cared for Thom. He was fascinated with the toddler's rapidly growing capacities for speech. Sometimes Steinbeck worried that he did not feel the great love that seemed expected of parents. He wrote that being a father was not unlike owning a puppy, with the exception that a baby is more intelligent than a dog. He felt that he could find the same intellectual fascination with any child that he found in his own children. He spent time teaching Thom Spanish as well as

English. When Gwyn brought John home from the hospital, both Steinbeck and Thom called the baby Juanito.

Two babies in the house proved louder and more distracting than Steinbeck had imagined. Adding to the complications was a continued decline in his relationship with Gwyn. The birth of John seemed to have drained her of all energy. She slept late each morning and spent a good portion of each day taking naps, leaving Steinbeck to attend to the housework and child care. When he returned briefly to Mexico for some postproduction work on the film of *The Pearl*, Gwyn exploded. Steinbeck returned to New York very much aware that his marriage was in trouble. In hopes of patching things up between them, Steinbeck planned to take Gwyn to Europe for a vacation. He hoped they could go early in 1947, after he completed *The Wayward Bus*. It became obvious to him, however, from the tenor of their arguments, that the vacation could not be put off for long. Steinbeck decided to increase the pace of his production and purchased a dictating machine. Rather than working slowly in pencil at one of his ledgers, Steinbeck dictated *The Wayward Bus*, then had his dictation typed by a secretary. The process made it possible for him to speed through the story, completing it in October.

By the end of the month he and Gwyn had left the boys in the care of a nursemaid and set out by ship for Scandinavia. Steinbeck had made the journey—on board the same vessel!—once before, with Carol, also in hopes of salvaging a marriage. For a while he and Gwyn got along better, the distractions of a sea voyage soothing their tempers. In Norway, Steinbeck was honored for *The Moon Is Down*, which, even as it irritated American critics and reviewers, had given great comfort to readers whose nation was occupied by the Germans. After a trip to Paris, Steinbeck and Gwyn returned to New York and their children.

Covici had set February 1947 as the publication date for *The*

Wayward Bus, yet when Steinbeck looked at the manuscript he was shocked. The book seemed to show in every sentence signs of the haste with which it was composed. *The Wayward Bus* was a highly sexual story in which Steinbeck hoped to present a true portrait of the difficulties caused by sexual tension between men and women. Reading the book now, Steinbeck found many of the characters to be simply coarse. Some of them struck him as caricatures rather than as symbols. His large ambitions for a cosmic story had failed, leaving him with a flawed novel that felt claustrophobic rather than expansive. He wanted to put the novel through another, more careful draft, but Covici persuaded him to proceed with publication as planned.

When *The Wayward Bus* appeared in February, it was obvious why Covici had not wanted the book delayed. Within weeks of publication more than 750,000 copies had been sold through bookstores and the Book-of-the-Month Club. The reviews surprised Steinbeck. Many critics applauded his dispassionate portrayal of the novel's characters. At the same time, Steinbeck's philosophy was once more overlooked. Sales of *The Wayward Bus* remained strong throughout the spring, but the favorable early reviews were replaced by essays critical of Steinbeck, his new novel, and his attitudes, particularly his philosophical view of the cosmos.

The success of *The Wayward Bus* did little for Steinbeck's marriage. Gwyn was drinking heavily, and their fights were becoming more bitter. Occasionally they would separate, Gwyn often taking the boys to visit her parents in California. Steinbeck, eager for a change of scenery, accepted an assignment from the *New York Herald Tribune*, for whom he'd worked during the war. The newspaper now commissioned Steinbeck to travel to the Soviet Union along with Robert Capa, a photographer who'd gained a large following with his combat pictures. Together Steinbeck and Capa would provide a series of articles depicting life in Communist Russia. The trip excited Steinbeck, and he spent much of the spring of 1947 engaged in studying the Russian language, Russian history, and Marxist economic theory.

The projected Russian trip was interrupted when Steinbeck was hospitalized. One of the railings on a second-story balcony at his brownstone had given way when Steinbeck leaned against it. He fell into his garden, breaking a knee. By late summer he was well enough to travel, although he still required a cane to get around. Gwyn accompanied Steinbeck on the first part of the trip, and they enjoyed a pleasant stay in France. By August, Gwyn had returned to New York, while Steinbeck and Capa traveled through the Soviet Union. Steinbeck was shocked at the devastation he found in Russia, grim reminders of the military might of the German Army. He compared his new observations with those from the Soviet trip he'd made with Carol a decade earlier. While Steinbeck and Capa got along well with the Russian people, both were depressed by the Soviet bureaucracy's regimentation of the people's lives. Steinbeck felt that the gray, totalitarian existence imposed upon the Russians reinforced his own theories about the importance of the individual spirit to the collective group. Back in New York in the fall, he began transforming his newspaper dispatches into a book.

Viking followed the success of *The Wayward Bus* with book publication of *The Pearl*. Steinbeck's brief fable about greed proved enormously popular, another of Steinbeck's short books about universal truths to which a large readership could relate. Gwyn was not impressed with her husband's latest success. While Steinbeck was in Russia, Gwyn's drinking had become chronic. Under the influence of alcohol she shouted harsh and abusive statements, belittling Steinbeck's accomplishments and abilities. Although he hoped that the marriage would heal, Steinbeck left New York not long after he returned. He went back to Monterey and used his cottage there as a base for research. It was history, rather than biology, that attracted Steinbeck now.

The failure of *The Wayward Bus* to live up to Steinbeck's ambitions had sparked in him a desire to return to the large novel of the Salinas Valley. He now spent days going through newspaper files, learning the most minute details of the history of his area. Steinbeck knew that the novel he planned would be longer and more complex than anything he had ever considered. He wanted every aspect of the book to be perfect and arranged to have the old newspapers photographed so that he could check his facts during the composition of the book. Pat Covici was thrilled to hear that Steinbeck was beginning serious work on "The Salinas Valley." The editor knew that Steinbeck needed large themes and stories to display his abilities and insights to their best advantage. Covici thought that Steinbeck should drop everything and write nothing but "The Salinas Valley" until he was done.

Steinbeck, however, needed distraction. The size of the Salinas novel frightened him a bit. He did not know quite how to start the book nor what structure would best serve the points he wanted to make with it. In Monterey he was able to resume his philosophical discussions with Ed Ricketts. They began to plan a new expedition, this one to fare northward. Ricketts was excited about documenting the marine life of Canada's Queen Charlotte Islands. Steinbeck shared the enthusiasm, and once more he and Ricketts began drawing up lists of supplies and materials for their journey. They had learned so much during the trip to the Sea of Cortez, and during their subsequent collaboration, that both were certain the new adventure would be even more fruitful and would produce a book even more effective than *Sea of Cortez*. Before Steinbeck left Monterey, he and Ricketts agreed that the new expedition would be undertaken during the summer. In March, Steinbeck went back to New York for a reunion with Gwyn and a hospital stay for the stripping of varicose veins that plagued his legs.

Gwyn was no more warm to Steinbeck than before. He did not share the brownstone with her but took a hotel room after his

operation. For all of the problems in his marriage and with his
work, Steinbeck was in good spirits. The forthcoming collecting
trip with Ed Ricketts was just what he needed to renew his
creative energies and bring some stability to his emotions. Steinbeck could already taste the cool sea air, already hear Ricketts
arguing some point of biology or philosophy.

It was not to be. Ed Ricketts was mortally injured on May 7,
1948, when his car was struck by a train. Steinbeck rushed from
New York to be at his friend's side, but by the time he reached
California on May 11, Ricketts was gone.

Steinbeck was devastated. Ed Ricketts had played so great a
part in the development of his thinking, had contributed so
much as teacher and as friend, that Steinbeck felt as though a
part of himself had died. He remained in California for a few
days, helping to settle Ricketts's affairs. Steinbeck went through
the papers and records at Pacific Biological Laboratories, de-
stroying those items which he felt might embarrass Ed Ricketts's
memory. When he finally returned to New York, Steinbeck took
Ricketts's microscope with him.

Gwyn had no sympathy. She cruelly taunted Steinbeck
about the part Ricketts had played in his life, accusing Steinbeck
of mimicking Ricketts's philosophy because he had no real ideas
of his own. Gwyn would not allow Steinbeck to move back into
the brownstone. She informed him that she was tired of the
demands he made upon her, that she wanted a divorce. Numbly,
Steinbeck established himself in a hotel and for a time lost
himself in liquor. The alcohol did little good. He felt cut off from
everything. The only source of comfort he could imagine was
work, but there was no question of proceeding with "The Salinas
Valley" in his present state of despair. He distrusted his ability to
write prose at all. In hopes of at least continuing to write something, Steinbeck resumed research for a motion picture about
Emiliano Zapata. In June he traveled to Mexico to make notes.
He began casting about in Hollywood for financing for the picture. Back in New York in August, Steinbeck signed formal

separation papers with Gwyn. The arrangement gave her custody of the two boys, as well as most of Steinbeck's income and holdings. Shattered by the divorce, financially ruined, creatively drained, Steinbeck returned as he had so often to the little cottage in Pacific Grove.

There, with thick fog wrapping the house, Steinbeck began trying to rebuild his life. For a while all he could write were long, self-pitying letters filled with mourning for both Ed Ricketts and Gwyn. A trip to Mexico in November failed to increase the speed with which the Zapata script was composed. He threw away far more words than he kept and ultimately abandoned every draft of the screenplay. Pat Covici's requests that Steinbeck return to work on "The Salinas Valley" went unanswered. Steinbeck spent some time that winter on domestic repairs around the cottage and the grounds, finding in his handiwork a craftsmanship now missing from his writing. He missed his sons terribly and looked forward to the following summer, when they would visit him. When the American Academy of Arts and Letters elected him to membership, Steinbeck wrote only a brief, cynical note of thanks. He ignored the Christmas season as completely as he could.

Winter gave way to spring 1949, yet Steinbeck still wrote little. The Zapata script continued to elude him. Everything he wrote seemed wordy and incoherent. He did not even like to think about "The Salinas Valley," which he knew would be twice as long as *The Grapes of Wrath*. His agents were concerned that Steinbeck might never resume serious writing, but no one could talk him out of his obsession with the Zapata script. Steinbeck spoke with several producers about the project. He grew close to Elia Kazan, a noted director who thought that Zapata's life would make a magnificent motion picture.

By early summer Steinbeck was coming out of his depression a little. He cut down on his drinking. Because of the Zapata script, he visited Los Angeles often. Steinbeck even went out on a few dates with, among others, actresses Paulette Goddard and

Ann Sothern. Steinbeck invited Ann Sothern to Pacific Grove for Memorial Day, and she arrived with a married friend, Elaine Scott. Elaine's husband, Zachary Scott, was a noted leading man. Steinbeck was instantly charmed by Elaine, delighted with her thick Texas accent—which came and went at will—and her lively intelligence and sense of humor. Within a few days he had begun sending her surreptitious letters and notes, to which she responded. The affair soon grew serious, with Steinbeck and Elaine arranging rendezvous in secluded spots. During one of their meetings Joan Crawford served as lookout. The affair was interrupted by the arrival of Steinbeck's sons in July, but by then both he and Elaine were deeply in love.

Steinbeck hoped for an idyllic summer with the boys, a season that might assuage some of the guilt he felt over leaving them. He spent long hours with Thom and John walking along the docks, sailing, going to the beach. On some afternoons Elaine Scott and her daughter Waverly joined Steinbeck and the boys. Although the summer was not without problems—Steinbeck felt that Gwyn was too lenient with the boys, that she was not teaching them the discipline they would need as they grew up—he was pleased when they remained longer than planned in California to avoid the outbreak of polio that had become epidemic in the East. When his sons returned to New York in the fall, Steinbeck was once more overcome with guilt.

Now, though, he was able to write his way out of his sadness. The Zapata script had finally found a backer: it would be produced by Darryl Zanuck at Twentieth Century Fox. Steinbeck applied himself to the final draft of the screenplay. Unexpectedly, a new work of fiction was also taking shape. It was to be a play, whose settings included the circus, the farm, and the sea, and whose characters were to be developed openly as symbols rather than as individuals. Steinbeck was fascinated with jazz and sought ways to transform that experimental approach to music into a piece for the theater. He played riffs on his characters, changing their identities and occupations at will. Steinbeck was attempting to write a modern morality play, in which his characters served as symbols of the human condition. As he began the play he called it "In the Forests of the Night," taking his title from William Blake's poem, "The Tiger."

In November, with the Zapata script finally approaching an end, Steinbeck learned that Elaine had left Zachary Scott. She and Waverly moved to New York, and Steinbeck joined them there as quickly as he could. They lived for a while in separate apartments in the same building on East Fifty-second Street. Steinbeck was pleased to be once more so close to his children and thrilled at the prospect of Elaine's divorce. His excitement served his creativity well. Early in 1950 Steinbeck completed his play, now called *Burning Bright*, the new title also taken from Blake's poem. Less than two months after he finished the play, dramatic rights to it were purchased by Richard Rodgers and Oscar Hammerstein, who planned an October premiere. Steinbeck, still making minor corrections and changes in the Zapata script, was nearly ready to resume work on "The Salinas Valley."

One more piece of writing had to be finished first. Viking was planning to reprint the narrative portion of *Sea of Cortez* as a separate book, to be called *The Log from the Sea of Cortez*. Although Ed Ricketts's contribution would be acknowledged, the book's byline would belong to John Steinbeck alone. Steinbeck began a long biographical essay about Ricketts that would serve as an introduction to the book. He allowed himself to ramble through page after page of reminiscence and anecdote, putting together a portrait of Ricketts that extolled his virtues without hiding his flaws. By the time Steinbeck was finished, his essay was one-fourth as long as *The Log* itself. With "About Ed Ricketts," as the essay was called, out of the way, Steinbeck was at last ready to approach the biggest challenge of his career. He was ready to write "The Salinas Valley."

NINE

EDEN

STEINBECK SPENT MOST OF 1950 clearing his desk of work. He wanted nothing to interfere with the composition of "The Salinas Valley." Steinbeck and Kazan continued to meet periodically, making changes and adjustments in the filmscript that was now called *Viva Zapata!* In addition to the motion picture work, Steinbeck was making notes and drafting scenes for a theatrical adaptation of *Cannery Row*, as well as working with Rodgers and Hammerstein on the dramatic version of *Burning Bright*. He and Elaine spent part of the summer in the country, joined by Steinbeck's sons. Steinbeck remained worried about the boys, convinced that Gwyn was not only neglecting their emotional development, but also failing to prepare them well for school. He engaged a tutor to help Thom and John brush up on their studies.

By fall he and Elaine were back in New York. Steinbeck's time was occupied with the final preparations for the premiere of *Burning Bright*. He felt certain that the play would be a large success and was equally confident about the prose version which Viking would publish as a short novel. In neither case were his expectations fulfilled. The prose version failed to sell to magazines or book clubs. Its reviews echoed what had become a familiar chorus from critics examining Steinbeck's work. Reviewers felt that Steinbeck had abandoned the social consciousness that had made *The Grapes of Wrath* and his other books of the 1930s so powerful and was now producing only self-indulgent popular stories for large audiences.

On stage, *Burning Bright* was an even larger failure. The play of which Steinbeck had been so proud in manuscript, failed to come to life before audiences. Steinbeck worked frantically during the Boston previews of *Burning Bright*, spending long hours with Rodgers and Hammerstein in an attempt to tighten the script and increase its effectiveness. The hard work did little good. The play premiered in New York in mid-October and received a thorough critical attack. No one had a good word to say for *Burning Bright*, and the show closed after barely two weeks. Steinbeck, furious at the critics for missing the point of the experimental, symbolic play, wrote an article that appeared in *The Saturday Review*, a literary magazine that was deliberately aimed at a large, popular audience. Steinbeck called his article "Critics, Critics, Burning Bright" and in the piece denounced the narrowness of most critics' minds. He stated proudly that he had never written the same work twice, nor even used the same form twice. Each of his novels was an experiment, and each was in turn attacked by reviewers for failing to repeat the successes of previous work. Steinbeck ended the piece with a gleeful promise to continue experimenting, to continue stretching himself and the forms in which he worked as far as his talent would let him.

Steinbeck did not spend a great deal of time lingering over the failure of *Burning Bright*. He had gotten a book out of the work and knew that the book would have time to find the audience that the play did not. Besides, he was about to be married for the third time and found himself so happy and preoccupied with the prospect of setting up housekeeping with Elaine that he did not have time to become too depressed. Early in the winter he purchased a town house on East Seventy-second Street, not too many blocks from the Seventy-eighth Street brownstone where Gwyn lived with the boys. Elaine's

divorce from Zachary Scott became final on the first of December. Three days after Christmas, Steinbeck and Elaine were
married in a quiet ceremony at the home of Harold Guinzburg,
the president of Viking. The Steinbecks began their marriage
and the New Year with a honeymoon trip to the Caribbean.
When they returned to New York, Elaine further endeared
herself to Steinbeck by insisting that his workroom be the first
priority among the many aspects of the house requiring renovation.

In February, Steinbeck settled into his new workroom to
begin writing "The Salinas Valley." For a few days he circled
around the opening of the book, mulling over the things he
wanted to say and the story he wanted to tell. As he circled
around the beginning of his story, Steinbeck arrived at a procedure that helped clarify his thoughts and provided momentum
for each morning's work. Pat Covici had given him a large ledger
filled with lined paper. Steinbeck began work each morning by
writing a letter to Covici, using the page on the left-hand side of
the ledger. The right-hand pages were reserved for the manuscript of the novel itself. He opened himself completely to
Covici in his letters, revealing his insecurities and concerns, as
well as his excitement over the big new novel. He felt in some
ways that "The Salinas Valley" might be the last novel he would
write; certainly he intended to put into the book everything he
knew and believed about himself and about the people of whom
he wrote. By the middle of February he had begun the novel
itself, starting the book with a long reminiscence of the Salinas
Valley as he had known it as a boy. The story would revolve
around two families, the imaginary Trasks and Steinbeck's own
ancestors the Hamiltons. Steinbeck himself would be very much
present in the novel, coming onto the page in the first person to
comment upon the book's characters and incidents. Soon he was
moving forward at the rate of fifteen hundred words a day,
putting in five to six hours at his desk.

Originally Steinbeck considered casting parts of the novel in the form of letters to his sons, and although he abandoned that plan, the novel was very much about fatherhood. In telling the story of Adam Trask and his sons Caleb and Aron, Steinbeck felt that he was working through some of the problems he was experiencing with his own sons. His letters to Covici were filled with comments about the problems the boys were having in adjusting to the disciplinary requirements of school, as well as with reflection upon the guilt he felt at not being present at times when his sons needed him most. He wanted to put into his novel all of the advice and wisdom that he could, in hopes perhaps that Thom and John might find in the book the lessons that they were not receiving.

Steinbeck gave the novel a sense of history and also imbued it with the special perspective about the human race that his years of amateur scientific and philosophical study had given him. He returned in the novel to previous themes and ideas, refining them now in the light of new experience. Although the novel is set in the late nineteenth century and first two decades of the twentieth, Steinbeck wrote from the vantage point of 1951, aware of the devastation that World War II had wrought and bothered by the materialism and consumerism that seemed the great result of that war. The battle against the Nazis, it struck Steinbeck, liberated Americans only to become consumers of shiny automobiles and appliances, their love of mass-produced things overpowering the individuality that made life worth living in the first place. At the beginning of the novel's thirteenth chapter, Steinbeck made his fears overt:

"There are monstrous changes taking place in the world, forces shaping a future whose face we do not know. Some of these forces seem evil to us, perhaps not in themselves, but because their tendency is to eliminate other things we hold good. It is true that two men can lift a bigger stone than one man. A group can build automobiles quicker and better than one man, and bread from a huge factory is cheaper and more uniform. When our food and clothing and housing all are born in the complication of mass production, mass method is bound to get into our thinking and to eliminate all other thinking. In our time mass or collective production has entered our economics, our politics, and even our religion, so that some nations have substituted the idea collective for the idea God. This in my time is the danger. There is great tension in the world, tension toward a breaking point, and men are unhappy and confused.

"At such a time it seems natural and good to me to ask myself these questions. What do I believe in? What must I fight for and what must I fight against?

"Our species is the only creative species, and it has only one creative instrument, the individual mind and spirit of a man. Nothing was ever created by two men. There are no good collaborations, whether in music, in art, in poetry, in mathematics, in philosophy. Once the miracle of creation has taken place, the group can build and extend it, but the group never invents anything. The preciousness lies in the lonely mind of man."

As his story grew through the spring, Steinbeck was drawn more to the Trask family than to the Hamiltons. He altered his novelistic strategy a bit, making the Hamiltons—whose story was his own history—as counterpoint to the story of Adam and Charles Trask, and of Cathy Ames, the woman who bore Cal and Aron, and who became a prostitute. Cathy's character was supremely evil, and even as he wrote the first draft of the novel, Steinbeck suspected that Cathy would become the focus of critical attacks. He had little doubt that his purposes in creating Cathy would be misunderstood; yet he hedged his bets anyway with an explanation of her nature:

"I believe there are monsters born in the world to human parents. Some you can see, misshapen and horrible, with huge heads or tiny bodies; some are born with no arms, no legs, some with three arms, some with tails or mouths in odd places. They are accidents and no one's fault as used to be thought. Once they were considered the visible punishment for concealed sins.

"And just as there are physical monsters, can there not be

mental or psychic monsters born? The face and body may be perfect, but if a twisted gene or a malformed egg can produce physical monsters, may not the same process produce a malformed soul? . . .

"It is my belief that Cathy Ames was born with the tendencies, or lack of them, which drove and forced her all of her life. Some balance wheel was misweighted, some gear out of ratio. She was not like other people, never was from birth."

By elaborating such thoughts so clearly in the novel, Steinbeck knew that he was inviting critical wrath. In one of his letters he wrote Covici of his suspicion that "The Salinas Valley" would be considered an old-fashioned, dated novel, filled with old-fashioned moral concerns. Yet Steinbeck was secure in the knowledge that his approach to the story was as experimental—as *new*—as anything he had ever written. Once more he was breaking fresh literary ground for himself, assembling a novel that was unlike any book he knew. The formlessness of the novel—as the novel grew, its various characters and their individual stories sprawled off in all directions, with Steinbeck allowing digressions to run for thousands of words—appealed to him. He wanted to create life on the page, not a dead but perfect literary artifact. The lives of individuals and families were rarely well shaped; neither would Steinbeck's novel be shaped and pruned carefully. It would grow and assume its own form, as though it were an organism itself.

Steinbeck was one-fourth of the way through the book by early May. The deeper he pressed into the story of the Trask family, the more clearly he saw the nature of the pages that lay ahead of him. He was telling a story that was biblical in nature. After Cathy abandoned Adam Trask to pursue her life as a whore, Adam attempted to build a life undisturbed by evil. Adam cut himself off as well from all that was good. The Eden that Adam hoped to create was no Eden at all, but a dead, stultifying life, the price for which was tragically borne by his sons Cal and Aron. Steinbeck was retelling the biblical story of Cain and Abel, using that story as a metaphor for the suffering that humans cause one another. It was a universal theme. At the same time, aware that he was writing a very personal book, Steinbeck changed the title of the novel from "The Salinas Valley" to "My Valley." But in June, after reading a portion of the manuscript, Elaine provided an even more appropriate title. She quoted Genesis 4:16: "And Cain went out from the presence of the LORD, and dwelt in the land of Nod, on the east of Eden." Steinbeck called his novel *East of Eden*.

Later in the month he moved for the summer with Elaine and the boys to a rented house on Nantucket Island, near the Massachusetts coast. Afternoons were reserved for recreations such as picnics with his sons, but mornings remained the province of the novel. Steinbeck continued to pile up manuscript, working Monday through Friday on the book and taking weekends off for reflection and recuperation. The work was exhausting and at the same time invigorating. He kept careful track of the words he had written, of the number of typewritten pages that were transcribed from his manuscript, even of the number of pencils he used up as he wrote *East of Eden*. At one point he estimated that the novel would require twelve dozen pencils to complete. By the middle of July Steinbeck had written more than 135,000 words, yet estimated that another 100,000 words remained to be written. When he was not working or relaxing with the boys, Steinbeck spent his time gardening or carving wood. His most ambitious woodcarving project was the making of a lined box in which the *East of Eden* manuscript would reside. The box would be a present for Pat Covici. On the lid of the box Steinbeck carved the novel's title and the Hebrew characters for the word *timshel*, which figured strongly in the second half of the novel.

Timshel ws traditionally translated as "Thou should," a command from God. Steinbeck, always the revisionist, always aware that "should" was a teleological word, translated *timshel* to mean "Thou may." The new translation, he felt, distilled the importance of free will and individual action. His characters, by the command *timshel*, might have made their lives better and freed themselves from their self-imposed tragic ends. That they did not was, of course, the tragic point that Steinbeck sought to make with *East of Eden*. As he began the final long section of the novel, he turned once more to monologue, telling his readers what the story was about:

"I believe that there is one story in the world, and only one, that has frightened and inspired us, so that we live in a Pearl White serial of continuing thought and wonder. Humans are caught—in their lives, in their thoughts, in their hungers and ambitions, in their avarice and cruelty, and in their kindness and generosity too—in a net of good and evil. I think this is the only story we have and that it occurs on all levels of feeling and intelligence. Virtue and vice were warp and woof of our first consciousness, and they will be the fabric of our last, and this despite any changes we may impose on field and river and mountain, on economy and manners. There is no other story. A man, after he has brushed off the dust and chips of his life, will have left only the hard, clean questions: Was it good or was it evil? Have I done well—or ill?"

Back in New York in the fall, the boys returned to their mother, and Steinbeck settled into the rhythms of the final section of *East of Eden*. He had to restrain himself to keep from writing more than fifteen hundred words a day. Steinbeck did not want the pleasure he had found in this novel to end. None of his work had ever given him such a sense of fulfillment, nor did any of his other books so completely fulfill the ambitions he'd held for them. *East of Eden* as he planned it would end in 1918. In October, nearing the end of the novel, Steinbeck informed Covici that the next project would be a second volume about Cal Trask, which would carry the story from the years after World War I up to the present day. It would be a book as grand and large as *East of Eden* itself. By planning a sequel, Steinbeck was able to overcome his fear that the end of the Trask story would be also the end of his career as a novelist. His spirits buoyed by the knowledge that he was not yet done with the largest adventure of his writing life, Steinbeck held himself to his schedule and in early November completed the first draft of *East of Eden*.

There remained a great deal of work to be done. The type-written manuscript was nearly one thousand pages long, well over a quarter of a million words. Elizabeth Otis and Pat Covici each had some reservations about *East of Eden's* discursiveness, and each requested major cuts in the manuscript. Steinbeck argued with them, making his own points about the novel's unusual construction, but he finally spent four months going over the book line by line. He rearranged some of the material he had written and excised some sections altogether. This work pleased him far less than had the joyous labor of writing the novel itself. There seemed to be little creativity in the editorial work, only an unreasonable fastidiousness and attention to form. Steinbeck even found himself cutting the long, heartfelt dedica-tion he had written to Pat Covici. When he finished the editorial revision in February, he was more than ready to take some time off from writing fiction. He and Elaine left for Europe shortly before the first of April.

They remained overseas through the end of summer, travel-ing to Spain, France, Italy, and England. The only writing Steinbeck accomplished was a series of travel articles for *Collier's* magazine. He and Elaine also visited Ireland, seeking out the original residence of Steinbeck's ancestors, the Hamiltons, of whom he had so recently written. While Steinbeck traveled, Covici kept him up to date about the progress of *East of Eden* from manuscript to finished book. The editor reported that he had never experienced anything quite like the Viking sales de-partment's reaction to the new novel. All of the sales personnel were convinced that the novel was not only a masterpiece but that the book would set sales records across the United States. *East of Eden* promised to be Viking's largest seller since *The Grapes of Wrath* more than a decade earlier. Covici scheduled a first printing of more than a hundred thousand copies. The excitement surrounding the publication of John Steinbeck's *magnum opus* continued to mount through the early months of summer. When the novel appeared, it climbed steadily to the top of all best-seller lists.

As usual, Steinbeck's predictions of a poor critical reception were borne out. *East of Eden*, reviewers pointed out in supercilious tones, was hardly a novel at all. The book was not so much constructed as it was stuffed together, a mad mixture of disparate elements that never coalesced. Steinbeck had heard it all before and tried as best he could to ignore the criticism. He was gratified by the public's embrace of *East of Eden*, taking what comfort he could in the knowledge that the readers who understood his intentions lived as he did, in the real world. Critics lived only in the books that they read and to which their curious and precious profession forced them to feel superior.

When he returned to New York at the end of the summer, Steinbeck applied himself not to a new book, or even to magazine articles, but to politics. He became involved in the presidential campaign of Adlai Stevenson, who was running on the Democratic ticket against Dwight Eisenhower on the Republican ticket. Steinbeck was pleased to have the opportunity to contribute his energy to a candidate who was both intelligent and articulate, two qualities not frequently in evidence among those who seek public office. Eisenhower was the great hero of World War II, and his appeal was in many ways patriotic and nationalistic, his image reminding Americans of the united front the nation had raised against the Axis. Steinbeck and many others felt that Stevenson sought to appeal to voters as individuals, presenting arguments and ideas that reached out to voters' intellects rather than to their emotions. Steinbeck wrote an introduction to a published selection of Stevenson's speeches and worked to help coordinate fund-raising events. He was disappointed when Stevenson was defeated in November.

With the 1952 election out of the way, Steinbeck made plans

to take Elaine to the Virgin Islands for a January vacation. The year had been a profitable one for Steinbeck. *East of Eden* continued to dominate the best-seller lists despite the critical reception. And *Viva Zapata!* had been one of the year's more successful motion pictures. Kazan's film starred Marlon Brando as Zapata, and both director and actor did a wonderful job of translating Steinbeck's script onto the screen. Kazan was delighted with *East of Eden* and even before its official publication date had begun seeking financing for a film based on the novel.

After the Caribbean vacation, Steinbeck settled once more into the Manhattan town house and at last picked up his pencil and embarked upon a major piece of writing. He did not, as he had once hoped, undertake the second volume of the Trask family story. Rather, he returned to the musical version of *Cannery Row*, which had been put aside as he worked on *East of Eden*. After several weeks of struggling to make *Cannery Row*'s characters and scenes conform to the requirements of musical comedy, as well as creating new characters and scenes where the pace of the play demanded them, Steinbeck gave up in frustration. The new scenes were more enjoyable than adapting the old ones, and they sparked Steinbeck's interest in fiction. After taking his sons to Nantucket for spring recess, Steinbeck began casting the new material about Doc and the citizens of *Cannery Row* as a novel, which he called "Bear Flag." Steinbeck admitted to his agents that he knew such work was an indulgence, but he felt that he had earned the relaxation the familiar material offered. Perhaps more important, "Bear Flag" provided Steinbeck with the chance once more to spend part of each day in the company of Ed Ricketts, at least in the form of the character Doc. Steinbeck knew that when he finished "Bear Flag," he would be finished with Ricketts and a part of his life forever.

In 1953 Steinbeck did not rent a country home until September, after the summer was over. He and Elaine found a pleasant house in the Long Island community of Sag Harbor. Steinbeck worked well in Sag Harbor, completing "Bear Flag"

before October and the onset of cold weather. He and Elaine
moved back to Manhattan for the remainder of the year and
began 1954 with the Caribbean vacation that had become for
them an annual tradition. Sag Harbor remained on their minds,
and they gave some thought to purchasing a permanent home
there.

With "Bear Flag" in the hands of Viking and also Rodgers
and Hammerstein, who would handle the musical adaptation,
Steinbeck was once more ready for a trip to Europe. This would
be Steinbeck's most extended European trip yet. Steinbeck was
giving some thought to a project about a modern Don Quixote,
and he and Elaine spent the first part of their trip in Spain,
trying to view the country as Cervantes had. After Spain they
moved to a large house in Paris. Steinbeck learned that Rodgers
and Hammerstein were lobbying for a change in the title of the
musical about Doc and Cannery Row, their preference being
"Sweet Thursday." Steinbeck approved the title change, and
Viking published the book early in the summer of 1954. Once
again Steinbeck made a strong showing on the best-seller lists,
and once more the critics awarded him a poor reception. Steinbeck was accused of exploiting material from his own past, a
symptom, some critics felt, of his failure of imaginative vision.

Whatever the state of his vision, Steinbeck did little imaginative writing during his season in Europe. The only real work
he did was a series of articles for the French literary publication
Figaro Littéraire. The pieces were brief and impressionistic
accounts of Steinbeck's observations of French life. Although
Steinbeck made notes for larger projects, he got started on none
of them. There were many pleasant distractions. He was more
respected as an artist by the French than by Americans, and
Steinbeck enjoyed the lionization he received as a result of his
work. His sons and Elaine's daughter, Waverly, joined the Steinbecks for the summer. Steinbeck as always marveled at how
much the boys had grown. Encouraging their independence and
self-reliance, Steinbeck sent Thom and John, who were ten and

eight, off on expeditions through Paris, and as far as Italy. Together, father and sons went for long walks, fished in the Seine, or took drives in the handsome Jaguar that Steinbeck had purchased as a treat for himself. They studied French history together, and Steinbeck worked to help Thom overcome his difficulties with reading.

The long, happy summer came to a close, and the children returned to the United States. Steinbeck and Elaine spent the fall touring France, Italy, and Greece. They sailed home in December, reaching New York in time for Christmas. The city continued to please Steinbeck, but he and Elaine also began looking for a house in the country, where they could escape from Manhattan's distractions. They found the house they wanted in Sag Harbor, the Long Island community where they had vacationed previously. Steinbeck's new house stood on a two-acre tract that looked out over the water. The house was solidly built, but Steinbeck immediately began working on it, using his craftsmanship to make many small and large improvements. He was pleased to be located once more with a view of a harbor and made plans to purchase his own boat. He was also making plans for new work. Although he knew that his critics—not to mention his publishers—would be pleased if he returned to books like *The Grapes of Wrath*, Steinbeck had no intention of repeating himself. "Sweet Thursday" had been an enjoyable indulgence, nothing more. Now he wanted to strip away everything he had learned about writing in his fifty-three years and start all over. There were experiments he wanted to make.

TEN

REDISCOVERING AMERICA

STEINBECK'S FIRST EXPERIMENT WOULD be a new novel, which he planned to construct solely from dialogue. He felt that by eliminating narrative and description he might achieve a book that would be as powerful and psychologically insightful as it was innovative. He worked on the book through the spring and summer of 1955, interrupting his effort in the fall when Rodgers and Hammerstein's musical version of "Sweet Thursday" began rehearsals for its winter premiere. After urging the new title on Steinbeck, the composer and the dramatist had once more changed their minds. The finished play was called *Pipe Dream*. Steinbeck felt that Rodgers and Hammerstein had removed all the rough edges and unexpected twists of character that made the people of Cannery Row interesting. He felt that *Pipe Dream* would be a successful theatrical entertainment but that changes must be made in the script if it were to give a realistic sense of Doc and his friends. Rodgers and Hammerstein would not make the changes. *Pipe Dream* opened and closed in December 1955, even a bigger failure than *Burning Bright*. Steinbeck and Elaine escaped the aftermath of the play by celebrating the New Year in Trinidad.

The dialogue novel was still on Steinbeck's mind, although he was beginning to suspect that the experiment was ultimately a dead end. He had hoped to capture in inflection and idiom all of his characters' history and quirks but found his format too restrictive. Such an approach might have worked on the stage, perhaps, but after *Pipe Dream* Steinbeck was through with the stage. By spring 1956, Steinbeck was casting about for a new project. Adlai Stevenson was preparing to make another attempt at the presidency, and Steinbeck was once more drawn to the candidate. Steinbeck's interest in politics, along with his recent stay in France, came together in the form of a short new novel. The book was a satirical fantasy about a French political crisis that resulted in the restoration of the French king. Steinbeck's monarch was whimsically named Pippin, and the novel was called *The Short Reign of Pippin IV: A Fabrication*. Steinbeck used his fantasy as a forum for humorous and biting portraits of all political parties, of organized religion, and of youthful rebellion.

Political reality attracted him in late summer when he broke off his work on the story of Pippin to cover the Democratic and Republican national conventions for the Louisville, Kentucky *Courier-Journal*. After the conventions he worked for Adlai Stevenson until the candidate was, once more, defeated by Dwight Eisenhower. Steinbeck returned to his desk and finished his book about Pippin in November 1956. Pat Covici did not care for the novel and was not hopeful of its becoming a commercial success. Steinbeck could imagine Covici's reaction to the next major project he planned, a translation of Malory's *Morte d'Arthur* into simple, modern English. His agent was opposed to the project as well. Steinbeck could not be dissuaded from the translation. The work would be a true labor of love and draw him back to the story that had been most important to him since his childhood. Because of the success of his books, as well as of Kazan's film of *East of Eden*, which starred James Dean and of which Steinbeck owned nearly 25 percent, he could afford to devote years to reading and research. Steinbeck thought that the Malory translation would take a decade to accomplish, and he was determined to do a scholarly as well as an artistic job. He spent the spring preparing for his labor, diverting himself with fishing off the coast of Long Island. He enjoyed a triumph over Covici's dire predictions when *The Short Reign of Pippin IV* was published to great success and Book-of-the-Month Club selection. Even the critics seemed kinder than usual to Steinbeck's new work.

By late April he and Elaine were in Italy where Steinbeck began research into medieval history. He wanted to develop a sense of Malory's times so that he could understand Malory the man. It was important to Steinbeck that he retain as much of a sense of Malory's hopes and intentions in the *Morte d'Arthur* as possible. He spent a large part of July in England, examining various translations of the Arthur story and absorbing as much as he could of the landscape over which Arthur had reigned and in which Malory had lived. Armed with new perceptions, Steinbeck equipped his New York home with a microfilm reader and obtained copies of rare manuscripts that he could study on his own schedule. He began drafting some passages, trying to use language that was as plain as possible but also seeking rhythms that would give modern readers the experience of sharing Arthur's times.

After a winter of research, Steinbeck moved to the Sag Harbor house where he relaxed from literary work by building himself a small, self-contained workroom. The one-room building was set near the edge of Steinbeck's property and was large enough to accommodate only himself, his desk and chair, his references, and his tools. Delighted with the workroom, Steinbeck proclaimed it his "Joyous Garde," giving it the same name as Lancelot's castle. He also worked in the compact cabin of his boat. Whatever his location, Steinbeck put in long hours each day. Occasionally he made notes for a novel reminiscent of *Don Quixote*, but his main preoccupation remained Malory. Once more he and Elaine spent the summer in England, where Steinbeck gathered more material and impressions for his version of the life of King Arthur.

His Don Quixote novel went nowhere, despite several attempts. The only work that excited him now was the book he was calling *The Acts of King Arthur and His Noble Knights.* Steinbeck's ambitions for the book had grown apace with his research. He felt that he was making Malory's material his own. The book would not be a translation, but a retelling. Working in England in 1959, Steinbeck found in Arthur the sort of character who he felt was missing from contemporary literature. Arthur was in many ways flawed, and in some ways a horrible man, but Arthur was also capable of facing his flaws and fighting to create for himself a magnificent destiny. Steinbeck thought that the writings of modern authors—and he included much of his own work—concentrated too much on despair and failure. Modern novels seemed weary with resignation and cynicism. Arthur was a character who was also a great man. His was a life lived fully and without surrender. Steinbeck began to think that *The Acts of King Arthur* might be the great achievement of his life.

In December 1959, Steinbeck's work was interrupted when he suffered a small stroke. Its effects were not permanent, and Steinbeck was sufficiently recovered by January to spend two weeks in the Caribbean. The stroke reminded Steinbeck, however, of the long decline of his parents' health and served as a warning of his own mortality. When he returned from his vacation, he put aside the Arthur manuscript. He wanted to return to work not in the re-creation of a distant past, but in an examination of the problems that beset his own times. He started a new novel.

Steinbeck's protagonist was hardly Arthurian. Harvard-educated Ethan Allen Hawley, once prosperous, now a grocery clerk, provided Steinbeck with a character whose moral dilemma approximated that of his nation. It was not enough any more, Hawley realized, to be a good human being, to live a life guided by sound moral values. Such a life was meaningless in a world ruled by avarice. History itself was portrayed in the novel as an item for sale, as was Hawley's character. Surrounded by examples of the commercialization of the modern world, Hawley surrenders to financial temptation, hoping to resurrect his once-prominent family name and fortune, even if he must resort to illegal means in doing so. Hawley's temptation and collapse are mirrored in the willingness of his son to commit an act of plagiarism in hopes of winning an essay contest. As the novel approaches its conclusion, Hawley is once more tempted, this time by thoughts of suicide. Yet as he prepares to kill himself, his innate goodness is resurrected. The moral weakness that led Ethan Hawley to the edge of self-destruction is replaced with a bright determination to fight back and redeem himself.

The work went swiftly. Steinbeck remained committed to technical experiment and, after the novel's two opening chapters, shifted his narrative to the first person, telling the story in Ethan Hawley's own voice. Steinbeck called the novel *The Winter of Our Discontent*. Although Covici, Elizabeth Otis, and even Elaine expressed reservations about the book, Steinbeck was pleased with it. Ethan Hawley's voice was his own voice, and Hawley's obsession with the degradation of history and the quality of American life mirrored Steinbeck's own concerns. *The Winter of Our Discontent* was set in 1960 and presented Steinbeck's vision of America as the nation entered a troubled decade.

He finished the book early in the summer but was not yet through with his rediscovery of his country. Adlai Stevenson, among others, had encouraged Steinbeck to travel through the United States as he had in the 1930s, gathering impressions and canvassing attitudes that Steinbeck could cast in the form of a book. The idea appealed to Steinbeck, and as he completed *The Winter of Our Discontent*, he began making plans for a drive through America. He commissioned the construction of a special vehicle—a sturdy truck on the back of which was mounted a cabin in which Steinbeck could sleep, cook, and work. He was delighted with the truck when it arrived, and spent much of the summer provisioning it for the expedition ahead. Elaine, concerned about her husband's health, was at first opposed to the trek. She could not change Steinbeck's mind, however, and christened his vehicle "Rosinante" in honor of Don Quixote's love. Steinbeck decided to take their pet poodle, Charley, along on the journey, which would begin shortly after Labor Day.

The first portion of his drive took him to the north of Maine. Steinbeck responded immediately to the countryside through which he drove, feeling the thrill that unspoiled landscape provided. After visiting the Northeast, during which Steinbeck got acquainted with the challenges of living in his vehicle, he and Charley set out across the United States. As much as possible Steinbeck avoided the superhighways, which he felt were all alike and offered travelers no glimpse of anything beyond billboards and artificially maintained shrubbery and sidings. He steered his course clear of cities as well, trying to discover what, if anything, remained of the nation in which he had grown up and built his reputation. Frequently Steinbeck invited people into his truck for a drink, but only rarely did he offer his name. He wanted to be as anonymous as possible, so that his impressions would be as honest as possible.

The long drive West occupied Steinbeck through most of October. Much of what he encountered disgusted him, but he also discovered that there remained a basic decency about Americans that permitted him some hope for the future. He enjoyed talking with people and tried to do more listening than talking. Elaine joined him in Chicago and again on the West Coast. He visited Monterey and the Salinas Valley but found them changed almost beyond recognition. The sardine schools on whose bounty Cannery Row was built were long gone, depleted by overfishing. The docks and canneries were in disrepair; suddenly Ed Ricketts was a decade and a half dead. California's agricultural valleys remained among the world's most productive, but Steinbeck saw signs of the depletion of the soil and of an overdependence upon chemical fertilizers. Even in remote spots during his travels he found trash left by people unaware that the earth's natural beauty was their charge and responsibility.

From California he and Charley drove to Texas for another reunion with Elaine, as well as with her relatives. Steinbeck was amused by the cheerful jingoism of the Texans, whose state seemed more like a nation separate from the rest of the country. After the family gathering, Steinbeck and Charley pressed on through the final leg of their trip, a tour of the deep South, which brought them into contact with a deep ugliness. In 1960 public schools were only just beginning to be integrated. The forced integration sparked tremendous hostility in states such as Mississippi, much as forced busing would in other states years later. Steinbeck stopped in New Orleans to witness the hateful performance of a group of women who had gained national fame as "The Cheerleaders." Each morning the women congregated outside an integrated school and shouted filthy words as black children walked to class, accompanied by marshals. Horrified and angry, Steinbeck returned with Charley to "Rosinante" and drove back to Sag Harbor as quickly as he could.

He began work on a book about his trip while his recollections were still fresh. In January 1961, he and Elaine were invited to the inauguration of John F. Kennedy, the newly elected president. Steinbeck was a fan of Kennedy's and hoped that the young president would restore to the country a sense of purpose and direction. During the inaugural the weather was bitterly cold, and as Steinbeck listened to Kennedy's stirring address, he held Elaine's feet in his lap, rubbing them to keep the circulation going. He joked to Adlai Stevenson that he would like to be appointed United States ambassador to the Land of Oz. Following the inauguration, Steinbeck and Elaine traveled to the Caribbean where he made progress with his account of his drive across America.

An expedition of another sort took him from his desk in March. Steinbeck was invited to spend a month with the scientists working on Project Mohole, off the Mexican coast. Mohole was intended to derive some of the secrets of the earth's geological history through the drilling of a series of holes more than two miles into the planetary crust. The holes would be used to remove samples of the planet's core. The precision and dedication of professionals doing real science captivated Steinbeck as fully as ever. Many of the geological samples taken were the first of their kind. Steinbeck was thrilled to be given—against all of the expedition's rules—a small piece of crystal from deep within the shell of the earth. He smuggled the crystals back to Sag Harbor and kept the sample in his workroom.

Steinbeck had some trouble resuming the narrative account of his trip across the country. Thom and John had moved in with Steinbeck and Elaine after Gwyn became abusive to them. Steinbeck did what he could to comfort the boys, but he realized that in many ways his own sons were strangers to him. His work was further delayed by hospitalization in April for hernia surgery. Steinbeck's surgical wounds were healed by early summer, but by then the critical reaction to *The Winter of Our Discontent* had inflicted wounds of its own. Steinbeck's new novel was not measured by how fully it had achieved the goals that the story made clear, but by how poorly it ranked when compared with *The Grapes of Wrath*. Steinbeck's deliberate and controlled use of melodrama in the story of Ethan Hawley was seen by some reviewers as merely the final, incompetent collapse of a once-great writer. The book's symbolism and the affirmation of life at its close were almost completely overlooked. *The Winter of Our Discontent* became a best-seller, as did all Steinbeck titles. The reading public continued to embrace and appreciate his work, proving itself more open to literary experiment than were professional and academic literary critics.

The novel's commercial success did not ease Steinbeck's depression. Elaine had provided him once more with a wonderful book title—*Travels With Charley*—and portions of the account had already appeared in magazines, but Steinbeck had difficulty finishing the manuscript. It was as though he had been drained of all creative energy. He was certain now that *The Winter of Our Discontent* was his final novel. He feared for a while that it might be the last book of any sort that he was able to complete. Still, he remained a professional, putting in regular hours at his desk. Each page of *Travels With Charley* was agony, but each page brought him closer to the end of the book. Steinbeck delivered the finished manuscript to Viking in the fall.

Unable to work, Steinbeck devoted himself to building a better relationship with his boys. Steinbeck made arrangements to take his sons on a cruise around the world. He hired a tutor to accompany them on the trip. Their first stop was Great Britain, where Steinbeck told his sons of Thomas Malory and of the Arthurian legends that Malory had turned into literary art. Both boys were bright and responded well to instruction from their father as well as from their tutor. Yet there remained a great distance between father and sons, which not even a protracted journey together could bridge. Nor were they able to complete their round-the-world trip. Steinbeck fell ill, and the boys visited much of Italy and Greece accompanied only by their tutor. Early in 1962 Steinbeck turned sixty, and the birthday along with his poor health combined to depress him. He wrote very little, and even his correspondence dwindled to a trickle. In late spring the trip came to an early conclusion when the family returned to New York.

Steinbeck's spirits were only slightly lifted by the wonderful reception that *Travels With Charley* received. Pat Covici and Viking were pleased with the manuscript, and the book became one of the largest commercial successes of Steinbeck's career. For once even the nation's literary critics were receptive to Steinbeck's work, applauding the book's humor, sense of landscape and people, and even its wisdom. Steinbeck's personality—at once crusty and tenderhearted—shone clearly through every sentence in the book. *Travels With Charley* was filled with Steinbeck's love of land, of nation, of fellow human beings. Much of the book was very funny, some of it poignant, and some of it— as in Steinbeck's account of the Mississippi Cheerleaders— frightening and powerful. There was also, however, an autumnal feeling to the book. *Travels With Charley* was the work of a man no longer young, but not yet aged. It was a marvelous performance that gave readers a true sense of Steinbeck and his country.

The success of *Travels With Charley* was only the first of Steinbeck's triumphs in 1962. In October he was stunned when he was awarded the Nobel Prize for Literature, the world's foremost literary award. Any happiness he felt at such recognition, however, was undone within twenty-four hours. The morning after the announcement of Steinbeck's Nobel, *The New York Times* carried a brief editorial in which the judgment of the Swedish Academy responsible for selecting the Nobel laureates was called into question. The editorial leveled at Steinbeck every criticism that had become so familiar, wondering in print why the world's most distinguished award was being presented to a writer who had written so little of consequence since *The Grapes of Wrath*. What little praise for Steinbeck the editorial held was backhanded at best. Other periodicals also chastised the academy for making so inappropriate a selection. Steinbeck bore the attacks with as much grace as he could manage but was furious at the publications for the heartbreak they caused Elaine. He and Elaine traveled to Stockholm to receive the prize and were not startled when *The New York Times* resumed and intensified its criticism. The *Times* published a long essay in which Arthur Mizener, a critic, not only disregarded everything Steinbeck had written since *The Grapes of Wrath*, but also announced that even that novel was filled with tenth-rate ideas, the work of a writer of limited ability.

The awards ceremony almost made up for the bad manners and failure of understanding on the part of the American literary community. Steinbeck was a hero to the people of Scandinavia, both as a writer and as a man. During the presentation address, the academy's secretary, Anders Osterling, broke with formality and addressed the laureate as "Dear Mr. Steinbeck." The presentation speech made clear that Steinbeck's work had reached and touched readers. The address cited Steinbeck's "good will

and charity" and lauded him as a "defender of human values."
Special praise was lavished upon *The Winter of Our Discontent.*

Steinbeck's own speech provided him with a forum far
larger than that of a newspaper editorial page, and he used the
platform eloquently. He spoke of the responsibility of the writer
to the human species and made clear his belief that novelists
belonged to a tradition that reached back to the earliest story-
tellers. Part of the tradition was to affirm human courage and
love. Writers, Steinbeck announced, must believe in the perfectibility of human beings and should dwell upon flaws and failures
only as a means toward the achievement of that perfection. It was
an elegant, eloquent speech. And it did not seem at all out of
place when Steinbeck allowed himself a sentence in which he
warned against attacks on real literature "by a pale and emascu-
lated critical priesthood . . . tinhorn mendicants of low calorie
despair." After the ceremony the Steinbecks attended a formal
dinner and ball, with Elaine being escorted to dinner by the
king of Sweden.

The Nobel Prize changed Steinbeck's life. Although he
continued to be hurt and bothered by the contempt in which his
work was held by most American literary critics and teachers,
the Nobel served as a permanent reminder that the people, to
whom writers must always address their work, appreciated and
venerated him. As a Nobel laureate, he discovered a new array of
pressures as well as honors. His mail increased far beyond the
point of manageability. Additionally, he received a request from
the government to travel to the Soviet Union as a sort of cultural
ambassador, speaking to groups of Russian writers and students.
Steinbeck and Elaine made the trip with Edward Albee, a young
playwright who had enjoyed great success with a drama entitled
Who's Afraid of Virginia Woolf? The Steinbecks and Albee spent
the latter part of 1963 behind the Iron Curtain, where Steinbeck
found that his work was more respected than it was in his
homeland. He enjoyed the exchange of opinions with young
Russians and made his own political and literary points forcefully
and with great charm.

In December, Steinbeck returned to a United States that seemed to be falling apart. While he was abroad, John Kennedy had been assassinated, and the murder left Steinbeck sick. Kennedy's widow asked Steinbeck to consider writing a biography of her husband, but nothing came of the project. The American press was filled with commentary that romanticized the dead president, comparing him to King Arthur, and his administration to Camelot. Steinbeck for a few months returned to his book about the real King Arthur but no longer felt up to the challenge he'd set himself. There was too much going on. The United States was gradually being drawn into a war in Vietnam in Southeast Asia. American campuses were the sites of increasing protest and demonstration against the war. The youth of the United States seemed in full rebellion against their parents.

Back from the Soviet Union, Steinbeck and Elaine were invited to dine with President Johnson. Elaine had attended the University of Texas with Johnson's wife, Lady Bird, and the two couples grew close. Johnson trusted Steinbeck's judgment, and the men discussed the nation's problems frankly and openly. Steinbeck perceived the conflict in Vietnam as a noble cause for the United States, in which his nation's military force became moral force in combat against totalitarianism. As early as 1964 many if not most of the nation's writers were turning against Lyndon Johnson, and the president welcomed Steinbeck's company and conversation. Steinbeck helped Johnson prepare several speeches, including his address to the 1964 Democratic National Convention.

In March 1964, Steinbeck received another shock when he was sued by Gwyn and the boys. The lawsuit sought an increase in the financial support that Steinbeck paid his ex-wife and his sons. That Thom and John would side with the mother who had abused them hurt Steinbeck very deeply. The case went to trial in April. Gwyn's accusations were heard by a judge who, after considering her testimony, awarded an increase in alimony only large enough to cover the effects of economic inflation.

Two years had passed since the publication of *Travels With*

Charley, and during that time Steinbeck had written very little for publication. His periodic attempts to resume work on *The Acts of King Arthur* added little to the portions of the book already written. For a time he toyed with the idea of writing his autobiography but ultimately decided to let his work speak for itself. The last major project of Steinbeck's life was a series of essays on American themes, written to accompany a selection of photographs that Viking had assembled. Steinbeck's essays addressed various aspects of American life—the land, the government, the people and their culture, the nation's future. Steinbeck railed against the commercial monster that he thought was devouring the heart of his country, and worried about the destruction of our natural environment. But he also perceived and set forth a hopeful future for the troubled country, believing still in the untapped resources of American spirit and will.

The book was to be called *America and Americans* and was not so much a summing up of Steinbeck's opinions and beliefs as a restatement of them. It was the last book he would publish in his lifetime and the first he had written without the counsel, encouragement, and friendship of Pascal Covici. Covici had been quite pleased during the summer of 1964 when John Steinbeck was awarded the Presidential Medal of Freedom by Lyndon Johnson. The medal was America's highest civilian honor and was, Covici felt, one more proof of John Steinbeck's contribution to the nation. Covici traveled to Washington to see his friend receive the medal and hid from him the fact that he was seriously ill. Covici died in the middle of October. Steinbeck was devastated, but controlled his emotions and delivered a touching eulogy at the memorial service for the editor.

The brief essays for *American and Americans* occupied much of the next year; as Steinbeck completed the essays, he felt something like a renewal of energy. Suddenly he was eager to resume serious work on *The Acts of King Arthur*, and late in 1965 he undertook a major research trip to England. In the company of scholars, he visited many great public and private libraries and was present at the discovery of hitherto unknown Arthurian material from the Middle Ages. He hoped to complete his King Arthur book in 1966 but found himself caught up in political turmoil instead.

The war in Vietnam had grown wider. In April, Steinbeck's son John joined the thousands of other young Americans sent to combat. Steinbeck arranged for John to meet President Johnson before embarking on his tour of duty. John's letters home from Vietnam painted a portrait far different from the president's position, which was that American military might was winning the struggle against the North Vietnamese. John told of a corrupt South Vietnamese government, of American military incompetence, of children orphaned and maimed by the conflict. There was, the letter implied, no prospect of an American victory in Vietnam. More, the American presence seemed to be making the situation worse.

Steinbeck decided to see for himself. He arranged to bring his war correspondent's credentials up to date. Having already written a series of newspaper columns for *Newsday*, a Long Island paper, Steinbeck accepted assignment as the newspaper's roving Southeast Asian correspondent. Elaine insisted on accompanying her husband to South Vietnam, and they set out early in December 1966. By the first of the year they had been briefed by the army and were in Saigon.

Professional military men won Steinbeck's admiration almost as fully as did professional scientists. Steinbeck was not content simply to accept briefings from military public relations and press officers. Instead, he sought out combat patrols and joined them. He accompanied helicopter gunships on missions against enemy positions. From the vantage point of one helicopter he watched American B-52s rain bombs on North Vietnamese installations. Everywhere he went he was impressed with the young Americans who fought so courageously for this country that was so far from their homes. He recorded his emotions in the dispatches that he sent to *Newsday* and was not surprised at the anger his pieces roused among the growing peace movement in America. Many writers attacked Steinbeck for supporting the war with which they had become disenchanted. Steinbeck's positions might have been unpopular, but they were his and he did not temper his attitudes at all in the face of pacifist denunciations. Someone, he thought, had to speak up for the brave American boys whom he met. In his columns, he celebrated the American soldier, not necessarily the leadership that had involved the soldiers in Vietnamese conflict.

From Vietnam, Steinbeck and Elaine went on a tour of other Southeast Asian nations, followed by sojourns in Hong Kong and Japan. Steinbeck finished his *Newsday* assignment and began considering a book about Vietnam. For all his admiration for American troops, Steinbeck was very much of mixed emotions about the American presence in Asia. Even before he returned home, he understood that the war could not be won in the way that World War II had been won. Americans might, he thought, be able to impose a peace upon the Vietnamese, but to do so would require a permanent American presence in Vietnam. In a meeting with President Johnson after returning from the war, Steinbeck urged the president to end the bombing of North Vietnam. Further, he suggested that instead of explosives, Americans should begin dropping medicine on the North Vietnamese as a means of showing that American concern was on the side of the Vietnamese people. To Elizabeth Otis, Steinbeck privately admitted that the war would prove to be a disaster for the United States.

Steinbeck never wrote his Vietnam book. While in Hong Kong he had injured his back. By the summer of 1967 his pain was so intense that he was unable to work. Steinbeck's doctors discussed the risks involved in an operation to correct his back problem and were not hopeful. Steinbeck's circulation was poor, his arteries hardening, his heart functions erratic. Surgery would be very dangerous. For several weeks Steinbeck lay in traction, but it became obvious that only surgery would ease his pain. The operation was scheduled for late October. Steinbeck made what preparations he could for the operation, trying to rest and gather his strength. He was cheered by the safe return of John from his tour of duty in Vietnam, then shocked when the young man was arrested for possession of twenty pounds of marijuana.

It turned out that Steinbeck's son understood things about the American military that his father had not seen. Marijuana use was rampant among American soldiers in Vietnam. Steinbeck's son had even written an article—"The Importance of Being Stoned in Vietnam"—which was scheduled for publication after John's discharge from the army. The marijuana for which John was arrested did not belong to him; that was a factor in the acquittal of all charges against him. But John Steinbeck IV was as outspoken as was his father and used his notoriety to urge the decriminalization of marijuana in the United States. He felt that it was hypocritical to punish young people for indulging in a vice that he believed to be less harmful than the cigarettes that could be purchased in any drugstore. Steinbeck could not endorse his son's views, but he offered any help that might be needed. He hoped that John would learn a lesson from the arrest and trial. But he also saw in his son's behavior and self-reliance an independence of thought and action that was gratifying.

Two months after his back surgery, Steinbeck was well enough to travel with Elaine to the Caribbean once more. They celebrated New Year's 1968 in Grenada and returned to New York a few weeks later. In Manhattan and at the house in Sag Harbor, Steinbeck was confined to a chair or bed, unable to garden or fish, much less to write. In late spring he had another stroke, and in July his heart began to fail. Steinbeck spoke bravely of taking Elaine on a sight-seeing safari to Tanganyika, although he must have known that such plans were merely talk. He was dying.

Even as his condition deteriorated, Steinbeck continued to think about the Arthurian book on which he had worked so hard. As summer ended, he thought of beginning the story again. His sons were much on his mind. Thom was now doing his own tour of duty in Vietnam. John was out of the army and was intensifying his campaign for the legalization of marijuana. Elaine seemed to be spending all of her time caring for Steinbeck, a situation that depressed and worried him. He knew intellectually that no writer could fully live up to the ambitions and hopes that he believed were the bedrock of the profession—to tell only the truth, to use carefully the language that was humanity's greatest invention, to add to the human race rather than to detract from it, to push as hard as possible toward the always elusive goal of perfectibility. But he had spent his life trying. And he had come closer than most.

John Steinbeck died in New York on December 20, 1968. His body was cremated. His ashes were carried back to California, to Pacific Grove, and were scattered onto the land and the ocean that had so inspired him and his work.

EPILOGUE
JOHN STEINBECK TODAY

STEINBECK DID NOT LEAVE a large body of unpublished works when he died. In 1969, Viking brought out *Journal of a Novel: The East of Eden Letters,* collecting in a single volume the daily messages Steinbeck had written to Pascal Covici during the composition of *East of Eden.* Because those daily notes were Steinbeck's way of readying himself for a stint of fiction, they reveal a great deal about the way Steinbeck worked, giving readers a fascinating glimpse of his creative process. The poor critical reception of *East of Eden* is made all the more poignant by the presence, in almost every one of Steinbeck's notes to Covici, of Steinbeck's awareness of his ambitions for the novel, of his hopes for the largest success of his career. Few books provide so honest a look at the effort and pain that novelists endure as does *Journal of a Novel.*

In 1975, forty years of Steinbeck's correspondence was gathered under the careful editorship of Elaine Steinbeck and Robert Wallsten, and published as *Steinbeck: A Life in Letters.* Steinbeck never wrote a formal autobiography, but his letters deal with the major elements of his life. The correspondence allows readers to see the evolution of Steinbeck's literary and social concerns, his marriages, his emotional ups and downs. Many of the letters, naturally, were quickly written and were not intended for publication, yet even in his earliest correspondence, Steinbeck dwells upon themes and ideas that would inform his fiction and nonfiction throughout his life.

One theme that can be perceived from the first letters to the last is the Arthurian ideal that so fascinated Steinbeck. In 1976, his Arthurian manuscript was published as *The Acts of King Arthur and His Noble Knights*. The book became a bestseller, and for once Steinbeck received respectful reviews. Although the book was unfinished when Steinbeck died, *The Acts of King Arthur* has a completeness that would be envied by most writers. In his book, Steinbeck accomplished a retelling of the Arthurian legend that was at once contemporary enough for modern readers, while at the same time honoring the language and the atmosphere of Arthur's times. *The Acts of King Arthur* was a major achievement.

Although there were not many new books published after Steinbeck's death, those which had appeared during his lifetime continue to attract and delight readers. Steinbeck's works remain in print while those of many of his more critically respected contemporaries do not. Readers throughout the world continue to respond to Steinbeck's stories and novels; he is a beloved writer whose works maintain their timeliness, despite the passage of time since their original publication. A writer may be paid no higher compliment than that, and it is a compliment paid Steinbeck in bookstores and libraries tens of thousands of times a year.

The visual media have also continued to draw upon Steinbeck's work. Since his death, *Cannery Row, The Winter of Our Discontent, The Red Pony,* and *Of Mice and Men* have been filmed or re-filmed. *East of Eden* became a highly rated television mini-series. There is little doubt that motion picture and television producers will continue to turn to the long shelf of Steinbeck novels and stories for material for years to come.

The chords which Steinbeck struck in his work, and to which readers responded so eagerly, continue to be important.

The plight of the poor and the homeless, the need to feel a sense of belonging, the delicate and beautiful ecological balance that could so easily be disrupted—all are as relevant today as in Steinbeck's times. Steinbeck was one of the first ecological writers, and it is an ecological note that perhaps offers the best summation of his life and work.

At first, Steinbeck had been able to write with a certain exuberance about the sounds and smells of industry. "Cannery Row," he said at the beginning of that novel, "is a poem, a stink, a grating noise, a quality of light, a habit, a nostalgia, a dream." Within a decade of the writing of those words, that dream had vanished. The huge schools of sardines on which the canneries depended were played out, devastated by overfishing, depleted by greed. One by one, the canneries closed. The wharf degenerated, its wood rotting, the windows of buildings shattered, its metal rusting.

The final cannery closed its doors and shut down its machines in 1972. Over the next decade the bustling waterfront was remade in a new image. All the stink and life were replaced by fancy facades which fronted fancier restaurants and expensive boutiques. The places where John Steinbeck and Ed Ricketts had talked, laughed, drunk, and worked became a shopping mall catering to consumers. The artificiality that Steinbeck loathed had conquered Cannery Row.

That conquest, though, was not permanent, nor even complete. Over the years Cannery Row has become more than simply another shopping center. In the midst of the stores and the restaurants there now stands one of the world's great aquariums. The Monterey Bay Aquarium, constructed at a cost of $40 million, has since the autumn of 1984 presented visitors with a living portrait of the ecology of Monterey Bay. More than 80 exhibits employ advanced technology to sustain 5,500 specimens of local marine life. The museum reminds visitors that living systems are all related to each other, interdependent and intertwined.

Central to the museum is a glass covered display in which laboratory equipment, a preserved squid, and a copy of John Steinbeck's *Cannery Row* are arranged side by side. John Steinbeck might point out that books are more than museum pieces, even today. But I suspect that he would also be pleased.

ACKNOWLEDGMENTS

WHEN I WAS A teenager, my parents' bookshelves yielded both *The Grapes of Wrath* and *The Moon Is Down*. More recently, those same shelves provided me with a copy of Steinbeck's Nobel Prize acceptance speech. My thanks, then, to my parents for introducing me to the works of John Steinbeck.

Steve Planson of Greensboro presented me with an important Steinbeck reference early in my preparations for this biography. My dear friend Joyce Earnhardt, to whom this book is dedicated, delivered other materials as the book was taking shape.

Ed Ferrell, Henry Morrison, and Joan Gurgold all contributed to this book.

My friend and editor Linda Cabasin has proved with each biography in this series the value of good editing. This time she helped even more in sorting out the complexities of material and interpretation that accompany any literary biography. She is an exceptional person.

And always my wife, Martha, and our son, Alec, kept me conscious of my responsibilities to readers and to John Steinbeck.

REFERENCES

FROM STEINBECK'S *The Acts of King Arthur:* "In considering a man about whom there are few and sparse records, there are three directions one may take to build up some kind of reality about him—His work (the most important). His times (important because he grew out of them) and finally his associates or people with whom he may have associated."

The records of Steinbeck's life are neither few nor sparse, but his advice is sound for any biographer. Steinbeck's work, read in chronological order of composition, shows his growth as a writer and as a man; his letters were especially important to this biography, as was his journalism.

The part Steinbeck played in his times is a matter of public record, and the newspaper and magazine accounts of Steinbeck still make fascinating reading.

Formal biographies consulted include the following:

Professor Jackson J. Benson's *The True Adventures of John Steinbeck, Writer* (New York: The Viking Press, 1984). This is among the largest and most comprehensive accounts ever written of the life of a novelist. In more than one thousand pages, Professor Benson displays a stunning range of research, along with an idiosyncratic but effective approach to organization. Wisely in a biography of such length, Professor Benson employs a relaxed and in some places almost colloquial style. His biography deals in far greater length than was available here with the years of frustration Steinbeck experienced after the completion of *East of Eden*. Throughout the biography, Professor Benson reveals his deep sympathy for Steinbeck. In those places where his interpretation is arguable, Benson's clear thinking and careful consideration impose the same demands upon dissenters. This book will prove invaluable to all readers of Steinbeck, as well as irreplaceable for all subsequent biographers.

A far shorter and less trustworthy guide is Thomas Kiernan's *The Intricate Music: A Biography of John Steinbeck* (Boston: Little, Brown and Company, 1979). Kiernan begins his book by relaying the disappointment he felt upon meeting Steinbeck in the 1950s. That disappointment is mirrored in Kiernan's account of Steinbeck's career. Kiernan toes the academic line pretty carefully, presenting most of Steinbeck's works after *The Grapes of Wrath* as failures. *The Intricate Music* is even more brief in its treatment of the final sixteen years of Steinbeck's life than is the present biography.

Richard Astro's *John Steinbeck and Edward F. Ricketts: The Shaping of a Novelist* (Minneapolis: The University of Minnesota Press, 1973) is perhaps as much critical study as biography, but because of the special focus of the work, I include it in this section of the references. The book is a thorough and intelligent examination of the relationship between Steinbeck and Ricketts and is filled with fascinating material about Ricketts's extraordinary life.

Equally specialized is Thomas Fensch's *Steinbeck and Covici: The Story of a Friendship* (Middlebury, Vermont: Paul S. Eriksson, 1979). Fensch draws upon a great deal of correspondence to produce a close look at the relationship between Steinbeck and his editor. This brief volume offers insight not only into Steinbeck and Covici, but also into the nature of American publishing during the years in which John Steinbeck was one of the industry's great stars.

CRITICAL WORKS

As SHOULD BE CLEAR by now, Steinbeck's work has not been warmly received by literary critics. The nature of criticism is, of course, the prerogative of the critic. But Steinbeck seems to have suffered as much from the failure of his critics as from any artistic failure on his own part. Steinbeck's critics seem to forget that one of the meanings of novel is *new*. Steinbeck took seriously the novelist's responsibility to make it *new* every time he wrote. But there is nothing new about critics failing to understand that.

The critical books that were helpful to me include:

Steinbeck and His Critics: A Record of Twenty-Five Years, edited by E. W. Tedlock and C. V. Wicker (Albuquerque: The University of New Mexico Press, 1969). This substantial volume collects a variety of essays dealing with Steinbeck's work and with the themes expressed in his work. Especially interesting are six brief pieces by Steinbeck himself, in which he comments sagely and with no little annoyance on the vulnerability of novelists to attack by critics who speak with authority while expressing only their own private prejudices and concerns.

A Companion to The Grapes of Wrath, edited by Warren French (Clifton, New Jersey: Augustus M. Kelley, 1972) is a book that is as much history as criticism. French gathers together both critical and historical essays showing the evolution of the social problems from which *The Grapes of Wrath* was created by Steinbeck, and the reaction, often violent, that Steinbeck's book prompted. Steinbeck's own journalistic accounts of the migrant camps are included in the book. *The Grapes of Wrath* remains today one of America's most controversial and frequently banned books—Warren French's collection shows that the bans are nothing new. This is a fascinating book.

The Novels of John Steinbeck: A Critical Study by Howard Levant (Columbia, Missouri: University of Missouri Press, 1974) is a book-length examination of Steinbeck's novels from a critical point of view more enlightened than is usual in Steinbeck's case. Professor Levant announces early on his belief that Steinbeck possessed "an abundance of every gift and craft the novelist can have—except an intelligent and coherent sense of what structure is and can do." While Professor Levant makes his critical points cogently, I believe he nonetheless imposes upon Steinbeck burdens of structure that the novelist was aware of and deliberately ignored.

There are many other critical works about Steinbeck, but as always the reader is on sounder ground by approaching Steinbeck's books without preconceptions. Steinbeck, non-teleological to the end, knew that his books, and any books, are best judged by their success or failure within their own covers. As the following list shows, Steinbeck succeeded more often than he failed.

THE WORKS OF JOHN STEINBECK

1929: *Cup of Gold*, Steinbeck's first novel, the romantic story of Henry Morgan.

1932: *The Pastures of Heaven*, Steinbeck's linked series of stories, which form a novel about life in a California valley during the 1920s.

1933: *To a God Unknown*, the symbolic novel of a farmer's relationship with his land.

1935: *Tortilla Flat*, Steinbeck's account of the *paisanos*. His first large success.

1936: *In Dubious Battle*, Steinbeck's novel of labor unions; the first of his major works.

1937: *Of Mice and Men*, the first of Steinbeck's dialogue novels; a major success both as novel and on stage.
The Red Pony, a collection composed of the first three stories of Jody Tiflin and his family. (The fourth story was published the following year and is included in subsequent editions of *The Red Pony*.)

1938: *The Long Valley*, a collection of Steinbeck's short fiction.

1939: *The Grapes of Wrath*, Steinbeck's novel of the Joad family.

1941: *The Forgotten Village*, an illustrated book reproducing

184

the narrative from Steinbeck's film about superstition in rural Mexico.

Sea of Cortez, Steinbeck's ambitious collaboration with Ed Ricketts on a volume both scientific and philosophical. This edition is handsomely illustrated and contains scientific documentation of Steinbeck and Ricketts's expedition.

1942: *The Moon Is Down,* Steinbeck's misunderstood novel about the German occupation of Scandinavia.

Bombs Away, a piece written for propaganda purposes, telling the story of American bombers.

1945: *Cannery Row,* the novel in which Steinbeck portrayed Monterey and Ed Ricketts.

1947: *The Wayward Bus,* Steinbeck's symbolic novel of the stranded passengers on a bus.

The Pearl, Steinbeck's brief allegory about greed and materialism.

1948: *A Russian Journal,* the account, illustrated with photos by Robert Capa, of Steinbeck and Capa's trip to the Soviet Union.

1950: *Burning Bright,* the novel version of Steinbeck's first collaboration with Rodgers and Hammerstein.

1951: *The Log from the Sea of Cortez,* the separate publication of the narrative account of Steinbeck and Ricketts's expedition; Ricketts did not share in the byline of this volume.

1952: *East of Eden,* the largest, most ambitious, and least appreciated of Steinbeck's great novels.

1954: *Sweet Thursday,* the sequel to *Cannery Row. Pipe Dream* was the title of the version that was reworked as a play.

1957: *The Short Reign of Pippin IV,* Steinbeck's fantasy of French politics.

1958: *Once There Was a War,* an impressive collection of Steinbeck's journalism from World War II.

1961: *The Winter of Our Discontent*, Steinbeck's final novel.

1962: *Travels With Charley (In Search of America)*, the account of Steinbeck's cross-country drive.

1966: *America and Americans*, Steinbeck's essays written to accompany photos selected by Viking. The last book published during Steinbeck's lifetime.

1969: *Journal of a Novel: The East of Eden Letters*, Steinbeck's daily notes to Pascal Covici, written as he composed *East of Eden*.

1975: *Steinbeck: A Life in Letters*, four decades of correspondence, assembled and commented upon by Elaine Steinbeck and Robert Wallsten.

1976: *The Acts of King Arthur and His Noble Knights*, although unfinished, an impressive modern rendering of Mallory's great story.

INDEX

Winter of Our Discontent, The, 162, 165, 168, 176
World War I, 23
World War II, 126–130

Zanuck, Darryl, 143
Zapata, Emiliano, 141, 142, 143, 144